SORT YOUR LIFE OUT

SORT YOUR LIFE OUT

3 STEPS TO TRANSFORM YOUR HOME & CHANGE YOUR LIFE

FOREWORD BY
STACEY SOLOMON

BOOKS

BBC Books, an imprint of Ebury Publishing
20 Vauxhall Bridge Road,
London SW1V 2SA

BBC Books is part of the Penguin Random House group of companies
whose addresses can be found at global.penguinrandomhouse.com

Penguin
Random House
UK

Illustrations by Peggy Dean

This book is published to accompany the television series
Sort Your Life Out, produced by Optomen Television Limited
and first broadcast on BBC One in 2021

First published by BBC Books in 2024

www.penguin.co.uk

A CIP catalogue record for this book is available from the British Library

ISBN 9781785948671

Text design: seagulls.net
Jacket design: Clarkevanmeurs Design
Production: Antony Heller

Printed and bound in Great Britain by Clays Ltd, St Ives PLC

Penguin Random House is committed to a sustainable future for
our business, our readers and our planet. This book is made from
Forest Stewardship Council® certified paper.

CONTENTS

Foreword by Stacey Solomon 6

The *Sort Your Life Out* Way of Thinking 13

STEP ONE: STRIP 43

STEP TWO: SORT 75

STEP THREE: SYSTEMISE 119

STAY ORGANISED 213

IDEAS FOR EXTRA STORAGE AND UPCYCLING 235

Resources 250

Index 253

FOREWORD
BY STACEY SOLOMON

I know from personal experience the absolute joy that can come from sorting your life out. When my house is organised, there are systems in place and I know where everything is, then I feel calmer, better in control and I've got more time to do other things. If I'm ever trying to get ready for work and the kids off to school when stuff is everywhere and the house is in chaos, I just feel so stressed out and trapped. Plus, every task takes ten times longer than it needs to. On the flip side, when the house is tidy, clean and everything is where it should be, I feel more relaxed and free. On those days, I get to do more of what I love, like spending time with my family and friends or catching up on my crafting.

Living in such a busy household with five kids and two dogs, and with both me and Joe working full time, we need to keep on top of things at Pickle Cottage as much as possible. We do this by regularly decluttering, by having systems for organising every room in the house and by sharing a cleaning schedule that we even try to get the kids on board with. Not every day can be a perfectly organised day, but because we have systems throughout the house, it never takes too long to get things back on track. And because everyone in the family is involved, and knows the systems, the house runs smoothly even when I'm at work. Or at least, that's the plan!

Me and Joe have put the *Sort Your Life Out* principles into practice in our own home because, well, if we didn't, the chaos at Pickle Cottage would be next level. I know how lucky I am to live in a home with a lot of rooms, but there's also a lot of us. With the kids all at different ages, each with their own clothes, toys, games and other stuff, it's amazing how quickly the house could get out of control if we didn't have systems for our daily routines.

The reality of life for most people is that both partners are going out to work every day while the kids are at school, and then the last thing you want to do in your precious spare time is sort through the junk drawer. It's easy for the clutter to creep up on you, so I totally understand how it can get to the point where you can't even move around in your own home without continually shifting piles of paperwork or stepping over the floordrobe. Life is hectic and we've all got a million and one things on our to-do list ahead of organising the snack cupboard! But the fact is that the average family home contains thousands of items that aren't really needed, and living amongst all this clutter can make you miserable and put a terrible strain on your relationships. But it doesn't have to be like that and picking up this book is your first step towards positive change. I know how things can feel impossible when a home is full of clutter, and you don't know where to start. In that case, find one tiny space and focus on that. Remove everything from that small space and then put back only what you need and what you love. And repeat. It's simple, but it works.

Whether you've quite realised it yet or not, there'll be an underlying reason why you're here now, reading these words. It's important to understand the reason why you want to sort your life out as that will keep you motivated throughout the three-step process. If someone said to me, 'Right, you're going on holiday in three days so you have to pack your suitcase and get rid of any clothes that you don't need,' I would suddenly find the time, ability and strength to be able to pack that suitcase because someone has given me a deadline, a time limit and – most importantly – a reason for doing it.

Whether you're tackling your entire home, a 'room of doom' that's become a dumping ground or a single junk drawer, no matter how large or small the space, the point of decluttering is to free up space, but also to unburden yourself from the weight of too much stuff. Organising any space in your home around a set of systems will give you back not just physical space but also time, energy and freedom.

I truly believe that there is so much healing in decluttering and organisation. When talking to the families that we help on the show, all too often I'm told how the levels of clutter and disorganisation are a constant source of stress, unhappiness and arguments in their lives. It's heartbreaking to hear how people like Claire, who we met during series three, would go shopping or do anything else that would delay her from coming home as she couldn't bear the mess and stress of the house. And Claire is not alone in feeling like this. Happily, once everyone pitches in and we sort their life out, they almost instantly feel the positive impact it has on family life – the weight they've been living under is lifted and they're given the opportunity to start afresh and, well, that just makes me smile.

For me, organising and cleaning is better than any type of yoga or meditation for lowering my stress levels. Once I get stuck in, my mind clears of all my anxious thoughts as I focus solely on the task at hand. It's like someone has turned the volume down on the noise in my head. Getting to enjoy an organised home is a great reward, of course, but I genuinely enjoy the process. If you follow me on social media, then you'll already know just how much joy I get from jet-washing our patio, or anything else come to think of it. It's amazing how much satisfaction can be had from something so simple as washing away a bit of grime. I get the same pleasure from a freshly made bed, a neatly organised sock drawer or a restocked fridge, but if I had to choose, then I'd probably say that my greatest passion is for a bit of DIY and upcycling. Pass me my power drill and hot glue gun, and I'm happy.

I love to declutter, I love to organise and I love to craft. Now, you might not come to love each of these things as much as I do, but I do want you to appreciate and enjoy the benefits of having an orderly home. That might be finally being able to invite friends round because you no longer feel embarrassed by the mess, carving out a dedicated space where you can indulge in your hobbies or having fewer arguments with your partner over who lost the remote. While sorting out their stuff, one of the couples on our show even rediscovered a lost engagement ring and so decluttering their home meant that they could finally get married.

As well as having more space at the end of the *Sort Your Life Out* process, another likely benefit of having an organised home is how it puts a little money back in your pocket. When you can see what you have, from pairs of pants to a packet of pasta, it means that you won't overbuy and end up with duplicate items or perishables that you never get to use before they expire and go past their best.

The *Sort Your Life Out* process goes beyond putting labels on containers (although that's pretty essential). It's about giving every room a clear purpose, making sure every item has a designated place that it's returned to after use and establishing systems within the home so that every room functions as it should, and family life runs smoothly. When we go into someone's home on the show, we work out how we can make the rooms make more sense, how we can put in proper systems so that the spaces are functional, and how we can help the family to continue those systems once we leave. Don't get me wrong, there are days when I can't face the tidy up and I'll say to myself, 'Oh, I'll do that tomorrow,' but I genuinely believe that if you have systems in place that help you whizz around at the end of each day, you can then fully switch off and relax in a clean, clutter-free home.

Another benefit to having systems is that every family member can help out as there's no excuse for not being able to put on the dishwasher when everything is clearly labelled and easily accessible, so it's far less of a chore. Remember, a home is run not just by one person, it's the shared responsibility of everyone and so the entire family have to step up and do their bit. Rather than making you a slave to housework, when you sort your life out it has the opposite effect – it actually frees up loads of your time so that you can spend it doing the things that you love with those you love the most.

I'm so lucky in that I have lots of help at home, not just from Joe and the kids but also from family and friends who look after the little ones when I'm working away and can't take them with me or shove a load of laundry on when the baskets are overflowing. Plus, I have No-Nonsense Dilly to keep me on the straight and narrow when it comes to decluttering! But I know that lots of people don't have that same level of support and feel as though they have to keep everything going all by themselves. Don't ever feel like you're failing just because you see all these picture-perfect homes on social media and think yours doesn't match up. Mum-guilt and dad-guilt is real, but what you see online rarely is. Most people only ever post the good bits and so it's important not to compare yourself as everyone's situation is different. And what's even more important, never be embarrassed to seek help when you need it. You just need to ask. That's been a big lesson for me over the years.

For anyone who is feeling as though they're drowning under a sea of their own possessions, I really hope that this book helps you see the light – or perhaps even the carpet – for the first time in a long time. By picking up *Sort Your Life Out*, you've already made the first and most important step: you've recognised the need for change and that you must reset your way of thinking. So, visualise how you would like your home to look and put our three-step strip, sort and systemise plan into action to make your dream home a reality and to stop feeling suffocated by your own stuff. More than anything, I want this book to help you fall back in love with your home again. You deserve it.

Stacey Solomon

THE
SORT YOUR
LIFE OUT
WAY OF
THINKING

The *Sort Your Life Out* process for decluttering and organising your home is explained in the pages that follow, but you may have already seen it in action on our show. It's designed to give those people who need it a fresh start. When a family comes together and follows the three-stage process of Strip, Sort and Systemise, well, the results can be life-changing for everyone. However, in order for all the techniques and tips to work, each family member needs to be on board, in the right frame of mind and ready to support one another. Letting go of those possessions no longer needed or loved is a liberating feeling, but it can take a while to get into that mindset and so you have to understand what it is that you're trying to achieve, to recognise why it's important for your family's future happiness and to identify what, if anything, has been holding you back.

If you think that you might need to make a change and reorganise your home life, ask yourself these four simple questions and tick any that apply to you:

❏ DO YOU STRUGGLE TO FIND WHAT YOU NEED BECAUSE IT'S NEVER WHERE IT SHOULD BE?

❏ ARE YOU WASTING MONEY BUYING THINGS YOU'LL NEVER USE?

❏ IS LIVING AMONGST CHAOS STOPPING YOU FROM LIVING THE LIFE YOU WANT?

❏ IS THE CLUTTER IN YOUR HOME AFFECTING FAMILY LIFE AND IMPACTING RELATIONSHIPS?

If the answer to any one of these questions is yes, then read on ...

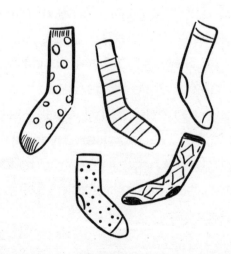

'THE CLUTTER DRAINS OUR ENERGY AND OUR TIME AS THERE'S ALWAYS SOMETHING TO CLEAN OR TIDY. IT'S TAKEN OVER OUR LIVES. IT'S TAKEN US OVER AS A COUPLE AND AS A FAMILY!

DAN, SERIES TWO

Why we hold on to things

Over the four series of *Sort Your Life Out*, we've helped lots of families who've struggled to keep on top of things at home. The one thing all of them had in common was an inability to let go of their possessions, even though it was often for very different but equally valid and understandable reasons. In some cases, those reasons were practical but, in other instances, those reasons were more emotional. However, for most people it's due to a combination of factors. Do you relate to any of the following:

☐ LACK OF TIME – LIFE'S HECTIC AND EVEN THOUGH I SAY, 'I'LL SORT ALL THAT OUT NEXT WEEKEND,' I CAN NEVER FIND THE TIME TO TACKLE THINGS.

☐ WASTE OF MONEY – I CAN'T AFFORD TO LET THIS GO AS IT WAS EXPENSIVE, EVEN THOUGH I'LL PROBABLY NEVER USE IT.

☐ FEELING OVERWHELMED – THINGS HAVE GOT SO BAD I DON'T EVEN KNOW WHERE TO START.

☐ EMOTIONAL ATTACHMENTS – THESE THINGS BRING BACK MEMORIES THAT MEAN SO MUCH TO ME THAT I SIMPLY CAN'T BEAR TO SAY GOODBYE TO THEM.

- ❑ <u>INDECISION</u> – I DON'T LOVE THIS SHIRT, BUT IT MIGHT BE USEFUL ONE DAY.

- ❑ <u>OPTIMISM</u> – I DON'T FIT THIS SHIRT, BUT I MIGHT SQUEEZE INTO IT ONE DAY.

- ❑ <u>OTHER HOUSEHOLD MEMBERS</u> – NO ONE ELSE IS PITCHING IN AROUND THE HOME SO, AS HARD AS I TRY, I'M LOSING THE BATTLE AGAINST EVERYONE'S MESS.

So, let's take each of these reasons in turn ...

'I CAN NEVER FIND THE TIME TO TACKLE THINGS.'

One of the biggest barriers to having a proper sort-out at home is never being able to find the time. Of course, it's hard fitting everything into a busy week: the 9–5, the school run, the weekly shop, the daily cleaning and then, on top of that, you're supposed to find time for a complete home overhaul as well. But just think about how much time every week you lose trying to find that crucial thing you really need but just can't put a finger on. Add up all that time over the year and you'll be surprised at just how many hours have been wasted wondering, 'Now, where did I put that ...?' All that time could be reclaimed and put to far better use, for getting your home in order, for streamlining your stuff, for designating a place for everything and for getting all those future hours back to do the things that you really love.

Think of your cluttered life as a computer hard drive – the more data (your stuff) stored on the hard drive (your home), the slower the whole thing runs and you can never find the file that you need. Deleting some files from that hard drive frees up space and then the whole thing works better, runs quicker and is a far nicer user experience. Just remember, you don't need to tackle everything at once in a single week, like we do on the show. Break it down into manageable chunks of time, so that you may only spend 20 minutes on one drawer or a couple of hours on a wardrobe, but all those mini decluttering sessions add up.

REAL LIFE INSPO

In series one, we met Kelly and Dan. They both juggle full-time jobs while bringing up their two girls and caring for Kelly's parents. When they converted their garage into an annexe for Kelly's parents, everything that had been stored there made its way back into the main house. Losing this extra storage meant that their home became a cramped and chaotic household. However, with Dan's job as a police officer keeping him busy all day and Kelly running not one but two businesses from home, there was never the time to tackle it all. Ram-packed with clutter, their house left them feeling disorganised, anxious and out of control. With all the family pitching in, the *Sort Your Life Out* team created a streamlined home that really worked for them and gave the couple time back in their lives. 'Life has changed a lot. It's now really easy to keep the house organised. My office is a dream. It makes me more productive as well because I actually like going to work now.'

'I CAN'T AFFORD TO LET THIS GO.'

When money is tight, we can be reluctant to let something go because it represents a lot of our hard-earned wages. If items are in good condition and have a monetary value, but you just don't need them or love them, then it's difficult to give up these things and admit that you've wasted a whole load of your cash. Be kind to yourself and accept that the money has already been spent and you can't change that now, so instead it's better to move on and value your space more than the cash you may never fully recoup. Certain things can be sold, and other items can be donated (see page 250). Getting some money back feels good but knowing that your donation is doing someone else a good turn is an amazing feeling.

REAL LIFE INSPO

In series four, we met Craig and his two daughters, Merywen and Wren, who were adjusting to life without their mum Lois, who had passed away four years earlier. While coping with the loss of his partner, Craig had developed an expensive shopping habit, buying gadgets costing hundreds of pounds, which he admitted was a hobby that went too far. The guilt of spending so much money on these gadgets for a temporary hit of happiness that never really filled the emotional void led Craig to block out their existence. Craig was naturally unwilling to simply let it all go. The reality, though, was that he was never going to use all of this stuff and so, despite the cost, it was time to resell, recoup some of the cash and free up valuable space that was worth much more to his family.

'I DON'T EVEN KNOW WHERE TO START.'

Sometimes feelings of overwhelm mean that we put off tackling a situation altogether. The most common feeling among the family members who we've helped on *Sort Your Life Out* was that they were daunted by the task ahead of them and simply didn't know where to start. The clutter situation had got to the point where they dreaded going home, sometimes even sitting outside in the car and putting off walking through the front door for as long as possible. But once they'd reduced their possessions and their home was in order, they all experienced a sense of relief, like a weight had been lifted off their shoulders. We want you to share those same feelings of lightness and freedom that result from following the *Sort Your Life Out* process. There are three clear stages to follow, which can be put into practice in any space, large or small. With the team guiding you through every step, we've made it easier to get started. Concentrate on one small space and then, once you can see some progress, all that clutter won't feel quite so overwhelming.

 ## 'I SIMPLY CAN'T BEAR TO SAY GOODBYE.'

Sentimental items are undoubtedly the trickiest possessions to sort through and let go of. When the reason you're holding on to certain things is a deep-seated emotional reason, then you may need support before getting started. This may not be a quick process, but it's important that those feelings are worked through as part of the letting go. (You'll find some suggestions for support organisations on page 251.) That said, it's entirely natural to invest emotion in material possessions. Often parents struggle to let go of anything relating to their

'THE HOUSE IS LIKE A SIZE 16 TRYING TO SQUEEZE ITSELF INTO A SIZE 10 DRESS. I WILL DO ANYTHING TO TRY TO STAY OUT OF MY HOUSE. I WILL GO SHOPPING OR ANYTHING ELSE THAT DELAYS ME FROM COMING HOME TO THE MESS AND THE STRESS OF THE HOUSE.'

CLAIRE, SERIES THREE

kids when they were young, not realising that by clinging on to those memories they may be negatively impacting the here and now. Whether it's keeping a selection of special items in a memory box (see page 208) or displaying one treasured heirloom in a box frame (see page 207), there are ways to incorporate mementos and souvenirs into the family home so they can be enjoyed on a daily basis without stopping you all from living life to the full.

REAL LIFE INSPO

In series two, we helped Aimee and Stuart to organise their home after upsizing from a flat to a house. As well as hundreds of toys for their three kids, Aimee had also kept hold of the chair she used when their daughter Mollie was a baby, even though it was broken and all their kids had outgrown the need for it. But this chair was incredibly special to Aimee as it was where she nursed Mollie following open-heart surgery. But it wasn't the chair that nursed Mollie back to health, it was Aimee herself, who still cares for her daughter every day. As the chair had done its job, Aimee could finally see that it was time to let it go. However, unbeknownst to her, the team took the fabric from the chair seat and had it upcycled into a cuddly teddy bear so that Aimee and Mollie still have a little bit of that chair in their lives.

 'THIS MIGHT BE USEFUL ONE DAY.'

Sometimes straightforward indecision is the reason why we hold on to an item. During the sort stage, we ask everyone to keep hold of only those possessions that they need or love, but all too often we hear the phrase, 'I want to keep this just in case.' But ask yourself this, just in case of what? Sometimes people hold on to an item out of fear that as soon as they let go of this so-far unused object, they'll immediately need it or that they won't be able to afford to buy it again. If that unlikely situation were to occur, how would you deal with it? If you don't use it, need it or love it, then that possession can be let go. And if you do have call for a similar item, it's highly likely that you could either borrow or rent one (see page 217).

REAL LIFE INSPO

As well as working full time and taxiing her two daughters to and from all their after-school activities, Rachel makes extra cash on the side doing dressmaking and wedding dress alterations. In series four, we helped her to reduce the 829 scraps of fabric in her stash in order to create an organised workspace where she actually enjoys sewing. First, we had to overcome Rachel's natural instinct to hold onto something just in case. 'I don't like to throw something away if I think it could be useful. We've always been a bit strapped for cash, so I don't like to think that down the line I might need something and have to buy it when I know that I've already had it and thrown it away.' But amongst the huge amount of fabric Rachel was holding on to were entire bolts of material that had never been touched and were unlikely ever to be used, so much of it could be sold on to regain the space needed for a proper workroom and make money for materials she would actually use.

'IT'S ABOUT TRYING TO HELP PEOPLE REALISE THAT THEY DON'T NEED TO LOOK BACK INTO THE PAST AT WHO THEY WERE, OR INTO THE FUTURE AT WHO THEY COULD BE. THEY JUST NEED TO LOOK IN THE MIRROR AND REALLY LOVE WHO THEY ARE AT THAT MOMENT AND KEEP THE THINGS THAT MAKE THEM HAPPY.'

STACEY

'I MIGHT SQUEEZE INTO IT ONE DAY.'

We've all hung on to a favourite pair of jeans that no longer fit in the hopeful optimism that one day we'll slide back into them, or our kids' wardrobes still contain toddlers' outfits when they've already started school. This might sound harsh, but anything that doesn't fit you right now doesn't deserve a place in your hardworking capsule wardrobe (see page 95). Focus on the clothes that flatter and make you feel good. And even though it can be a wrench admitting that they're growing up so fast, we can't afford to give valuable cupboard space to kids' clothes that are no longer age-appropriate.

 'NO ONE ELSE EVER TIDIES UP AFTER THEMSELVES.'

Your partner makes themself a cup of coffee, but the milk never finds its way back into the fridge and the teaspoon is left on the countertop sat in a tiny puddle. Your kid empties out their entire toy box to find that one particular action figure, only to play with it for five minutes and then get distracted by something else, leaving all the other toys strewn over the floor. You spend a couple of hours washing, drying and folding laundry, which is left on the step for the next person to take upstairs, yet the pile sits there for days. Do any of these scenarios sound familiar? Some people are naturally messy and so need nudging in the right direction. You have to help them to help yourself. This is when a system for everything around the house is invaluable. (Rule number one: no one ever goes upstairs empty-handed!) When everything has a place and each family member understands the system, it makes it so much easier for everyone to do their bit. A disorganised home can have such a negative impact on family life because, when you're tripping over piles of stuff and can never find what you need, it's easy to become irritable with others and start bickering over whose fault it all is. If you don't sort your life out, you could find yourself falling out with your family and falling out of love with your home.

Coping with grief while decluttering

Following a bereavement, it's hard to discard someone else's possessions while you're grieving. This is one situation in which there's absolutely no need to rush into making any snap decisions. For so many people, coming to terms with what has happened is a gradual process, so take the time you need to process your loss. It's entirely usual to find comfort in being surrounded by a loved one's things. Simply holding something that they once touched can make you feel almost as close as when they were alive. Letting go of an item can seem like an acceptance of their loss, that you're forgetting them or even that you're disrespecting their memory, but this simply isn't the case. You need to recognise that you cannot hold on to everything, as being continuously surrounded by memories of the past may be stopping you from enjoying your future. If your loved one knew the turmoil that holding on to their possessions was causing, then they'd undoubtedly give their blessing to letting things go.

When clearing someone's home, the temptation is to put everything into boxes and defer the decisions on what to discard because they feel too hard. When the time does come, take a moment to remember your loved one and recall what they truly cherished and what meant the most to them. Depending on how much space you have, focus on a few really important objects that clearly speak of them and their personality, and which you want to keep and treasure, rather than feel pressured into discarding everything. Try to let go of those things that no longer serve a purpose, instead concentrating on the best or most significant items that you'll cherish in the same way that they did.

REAL LIFE INSPO

When we visited the Smith family's home in series two, Raaj was struggling to let go of her late sister's possessions. With the support of her family and the *Sort Your Life Out* team, Raaj was able to let go of so many things that she'd been holding on to in order to keep her sister Harsharan close, even though the family were struggling with too much stuff and not enough space after the two households merged. After letting go of her clothes and many other possessions, the key items that Raaj kept were the empty spice jars that Harsharan cooked with every day, now refilled and in their designated place in the kitchen cupboards. These simple jars with no monetary value are in fact priceless in the way that they keep the two sisters connected. 'For a very, very long time, since my sister Hasharan passed away, I was holding on to so many things and I didn't know where to begin. Doing this together as a family, I feel something inside me has just been lifted.'

'THERE'LL BE SO MANY REASONS WHY PEOPLE CAN'T LET GO OF THINGS, BUT IF IT CAN BE RECYCLED OR GO TO A BETTER HOME, LETTING GO CAN BE ONE OF THE BIGGEST, MOST JOYOUS THINGS THAT YOU EVER DO.'

STACEY

The power of letting go

We've all been led to believe that accumulating lots of possessions equates to being wealthy. But what if all of these things that you own are actually impoverishing your life rather than enriching it? If you accumulate too much stuff without adequate storage, you'll quickly reach the tipping point where clutter builds up and the sheer volume of your possessions can weigh you down and have a detrimental effect on your well-being and your relationships.

When letting go, it's important not to focus on what you're losing from your life but to think about how shedding that volume of stuff will enhance your day-to-day. Discarding a high percentage of your possessions might seem like a daunting task at first, but you'll soon discover that it can be thoroughly therapeutic. Once you adopt the *Sort Your Life Out* way of thinking, you'll find that letting go of your stuff is liberating. By getting rid of possessions that no longer serve a purpose, you are released from the past that you've been holding on to and you're free to embark on a new beginning.

 ## WHEN UNTIDINESS INDICATES DEEPER ISSUES

There are some people for whom a thorough sort-out is not going to give them all the help they need. If a home is more than a little bit untidy and showing traits of hoarding or another disorder, it may point to deeper psychological issues. If you feel the time has come to seek professional and even medical help, as well as the support of your loved ones, you'll find the contact details of some support organisations on page 251.

The *Sort Your Life Out* process

You've already made the first important move towards improving your family's home life by picking up this book. The fact that you're reading these words right now means that you're ready for significant change. To introduce order where there was once chaos and follow the *Sort Your Life Out* process. If you work through the three main steps outlined in the following chapters, you'll strip, sort and systemise, with plenty of decluttering, cleaning and organising too, and at the end of the process, you'll appreciate the space that has been freed up, reconnect with each possession that you've deliberately decided to keep, introduce systems to keep each room organised and fall back in love with your own home.

Boiled down to its very essence, the three-step *Sort Your Life Out* process is:

1. <u>STRIP</u> – EMPTY YOUR SPACE, LEAVING NOTHING BEHIND, AND THEN CLEAN EVERYTHING.

2. <u>SORT</u> – CHOOSE ONLY WHAT YOU REALLY NEED OR ABSOLUTELY LOVE, THEN LET GO OF THE REST.

3. <u>SYSTEMISE</u> – FIND A HOME FOR EVERY ITEM AND ALWAYS RETURN IT TO THAT PLACE.

THE CHERRET—YAKU FAMILY, SORT YOUR LIFE OUT SPECIAL

* Over 60 obsolete chargers

* 11 old mobile phones

* 1,567 books

* 225 DVDs

* 23 pairs of swimming googles

* Nearly 3,000 toys

* 143 wedding cards and 90 RSVPs

* 17 packets of confetti

Our tried-and-tested process is a cost-effective way to improve your home life. In fact, it doesn't need to cost anything at all, but the positive change it will bring is priceless. We don't pretend that it's always going to be easy – sometimes there might be squabbles, struggles and tears shed – but to set you up for success, here are our golden rules:

The golden rules

1. ONLY KEEP WHAT YOU CAN STORE

We ask most of the families we help on *Sort Your Life Out* to let go of at least fifty per cent of their possessions, but in particularly cluttered homes it has been as much as seventy or eighty per cent. We encourage our families to halve the stuff they have to double their space at home. The number of possessions that you'll need to let go of will depend entirely on the amount of stuff you own and the available storage you have. If you keep more stuff than you actually have space for, clutter will creep back in and you'll struggle to keep your home tidy and organised.

You need to be able to see all your things, so you always know what you have and everything is easy to access when you need it. With that in mind, base the number of items that you decide to keep on the space you have to store them comfortably, then the goal is to let go of the rest. You don't need to dispense with everything you own to live a minimalist existence and we're not aiming for a soul-less, empty space. We're aiming for enough space to create a calm but welcoming environment, and to showcase those possessions that you choose to keep because they really mean something to you. The aim is to clear the decks by reducing the amount of clutter, then bring order and harmony to your home.

2. DON'T BARTER TO KEEP MORE

Let's imagine that the family is sorting out their shoes and the goal is to reduce everything in the cupboard by half. Now, just because your partner or kids are happy to lose more than half of their shoes, that doesn't mean you can keep a few extra pairs. If the target has been set for everyone based on the available storage space, then be strict on that goal in each and every category – it's only fair. If you start to trade off, you're opening the door to everyone keeping too many things here, there and everywhere and you may jeopardise the entire process.

 ## 3. HAVE A VISION FOR YOUR SPACE

If you keep a clear goal for your home in mind, you'll find it easier to stay motivated and see the process through to the end. This could be a photo clipped from an interiors magazine or an inspo pic you've saved on Pinterest. If you can visualise the end result and its benefits, which is a well-ordered home and a happier family, then you're more likely to succeed.

 ## 4. SET YOURSELF A CLEAR DEADLINE

For every home we strip, sort and systemise in our show, we only ever give ourselves seven days to complete the transformation. Nothing focuses the mind quite like a looming deadline, and so we stick to a tight schedule – there are times when it feels almost impossible, but everyone pitches in and somehow we always make it. The reason we give ourselves a limited amount of time is because when things are left open-ended, they have a greater tendency to drift. Setting yourself a clear deadline helps to get the job done. If you have a couple of hours free, focus on sorting out the bathroom, editing your wardrobe or sifting through the kids' toys. Then whenever you have an odd 20 minutes spare, declutter and organise a single kitchen drawer or cupboard. If you can find a spare 20 minutes every day, then pretty soon you'll have organised the entire kitchen. Larger spaces, like the loft or shed, will take longer, perhaps an entire day or weekend, so adjust the deadline according to the scale of the task ahead.

 ## 5. GIVE YOURSELF A REASON

As well as concentrating on the deadline, focus on the main reasons why you're doing all of this. The end goal that you're visualising may be the image of a clutter-free home, but that is only the 'what'. Write out a list of all the 'whys' as they are likely to be even more powerful. It might be that you'd like your kids to invite their friends over without feeling embarrassed about where they live. It could be that you'd like to have more time to rediscover the hobby you were once passionate about. Or it could be that you've lost your sense of self along with your confidence and now it's finally time to get that back. Once you can fully understand how this process is going to change your life for the better, then you're far more likely to finish the task.

'IF YOU'RE NOT SPENDING TIME WITH YOUR FAMILY, WHAT'S IT ALL FOR? THEY'RE SO PRECIOUS, THESE MOMENTS WITH THE PEOPLE THAT WE LOVE, THAT IT'S PROBABLY ONE OF THE BIGGEST REASONS TO EMBARK ON A PROCESS LIKE THIS.'

STACEY

> ### REAL LIFE INSPO
>
> When Sue appeared in series two, she had lived in her house for 40 years. After caring for her elderly mum for almost 20 years, Sue was left feeling lost and overwhelmed. The levels of clutter at Sue's house had reached the stage where it was unsafe for any of her six beloved grandchildren to visit, so Sue was missing out on spending quality time with all of them. Her daughters were desperate to get Sue the help she needed around the home, but only at this point was she ready to accept that help. Sue had realised that she'd much rather have her grand-children surrounding her than 40 years' worth of clutter.

6. WORK AS A TEAM

Don't feel that you have to do all of this on your own, it's perfectly fine to ask for help. If you're tackling the family home together, then make sure every member participates in the sorting process. If you live alone, buddy up with a friend whose opinion you trust and get their thoughts on what you should keep and what you ought to discard. When it comes to items that you struggle to let go of emotionally, you may find that taking some time out to chat through the reasons why you've held on to them with a friend is a healing step towards being able to let go. Your sorting buddy won't have the same emotional investment in your possessions and can offer their perspective, which may just ease the pain and speed up the sorting process. And a fresh pair of eyes can see the practicalities and possibilities of your space, whereas you've probably become a bit blind to it all.

> ## REAL LIFE INSPO
>
> Following her divorce, Steph threw herself into raising her three happy, healthy daughters and so the house slipped down her list of priorities. A strong, independent woman, Steph had built up barriers around the idea that she needed to do it all herself and, as a consequence, she found it hard to ask for help. By the time we met Steph and her family in series one, the clutter in the house had reached the stage when it had to be tackled. Steph found the strength to admit that she did need help and couldn't do it all on her own. Of course, she didn't have to as we were there to help.

 ## 7. KEEP GOING, IT'LL BE WORTH IT

There may be a point during the sorting stage when you want to give up. That's normal. As the saying goes, things always seem to get worse before they get better. Our brains prefer things to feel familiar and predictable, which means they don't like change, and your family is trying to make some big changes here, so everyone needs to dig deep. Keep in mind that your home contains a finite amount of stuff – even if it's loads of stuff – and so there's always a limit to it and the decluttering process will come to an end. Once you've successfully finished sorting through a few of the categories of items, you'll start to feel more confident in your decision-making. And when that last possession is either kept, sold, donated or recycled, you'll be a giant step closer to your dream home.

'THE HOUSE IS GIVING
US THE OPPORTUNITY
NOW TO BE A FAMILY.
I LOVE THE POSITIVITY
THAT HAS COME WITH
THIS PROCESS, THE JOY
OF ACTUALLY SAYING
GOODBYE TO SOMETHING
AND MOVING ON.'

DANIELA, SERIES FOUR

8. NEVER SACRIFICE SANDWICH TIME!

The *Sort Your Life Out* process can get hectic and so you'll need to keep your energy levels up throughout every stage. Whenever you feel like your blood sugar levels have dropped right down and you need to take a quiet moment out, just sit down and have a sandwich.

Keep these pages marked so that you can flip back to the golden rules whenever you need a boost of motivation over the coming stages. When we work with our families during the *Sort Your Life Out* process, day one of the strip stage in the warehouse is as much about getting into the right mindset as it is about how much stuff is being let go. All too often, your sense of self can become buried underneath all the stuff, so the process of letting go of possessions can stir up strong emotions, but it can also lead you to rediscover who you are and what you want from family life.

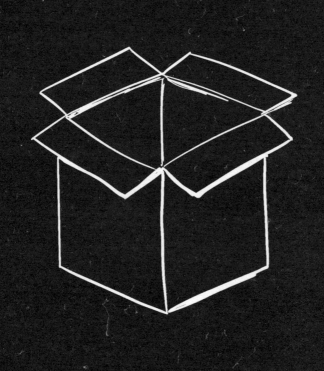

STEP ONE

STRIP

Whenever we help a family on the show, the very first step we take is to strip their home right back to its bare bones and transport all the items – from the biggest super king bed to the smallest toothbrush – to a giant space ready for sorting. We clear the entire space for a number of reasons. Firstly, once all their possessions are boxed up, everything can be conveniently moved around and similar items can be grouped together ready for sorting. Secondly, when the home is completely empty, it's far easier to see just how much available space there is and how it can be best put to use. It enables us to assess any existing storage, highlight ways in which we can maximise the space and then calculate what percentage of possessions the family needs to lose. And thirdly, it's so much better to clean and decorate an empty space without loads of stuff in the way to trip over.

That's how we do it on the show, but come on, who in real life has access to a 10,000 square foot warehouse? Let's be practical: stripping your entire home in one go and laying out every single one of your possessions in the same way that we do just isn't an option. But that doesn't matter and it shouldn't stop you from sorting your life out. You'll just need to work within the space available to you. So, rather than attempting to empty your home and box up all your possessions, it's fine to start small and keep things manageable. You could start with a single junk drawer, or a kitchen cupboard or a wardrobe, or you might plunge in and tackle one whole room. Whichever space you choose, keep in mind that once every item is laid out across the floor, it'll take up a surprising amount of space.

When it comes to sorting your stuff, for the best results it's preferable to sort items by category so that you're looking at all the similar things at once. Everything that we own can be divided into some basic categories in order to make the stripping, sorting and letting go process easier.

The items that most of us have in our homes can be allocated to one of the following categories:

- ❏ CLOTHES, ACCESSORIES AND SHOES
- ❏ TOILETRIES, MAKE-UP AND SCENTS
- ❏ KITCHENWARE
- ❏ PERISHABLE FOOD ITEMS
- ❏ CLEANING PRODUCTS
- ❏ TOWELS, BED LINENS AND BLANKETS
- ❏ BOOKS
- ❏ ELECTRONIC DEVICES, DVDS AND/OR CDS
- ❏ PAPERWORK
- ❏ CHILDREN'S TOYS
- ❏ LEISURE ITEMS
- ❏ PHOTOGRAPHS
- ❏ SENTIMENTAL OBJECTS

'I KNOW THAT NOT EVERYONE HAS A WAREHOUSE, BUT THE PRINCIPLE STILL APPLIES, EVEN IN THE SMALLEST OF SPACES. SO, IF YOU'RE LOOKING AT ONE CUPBOARD, FOR EXAMPLE, TAKE EVERYTHING OUT, LAY IT ALL OUT ACROSS THE FLOOR AND SEE WHAT YOU HAVE. THEN ASK YOURSELF, 'IS ALL OF THIS GOING TO SERVE ME A PURPOSE?'

STACEY

If you can, gather together every object in that category so they're all in front of you at the same time. If you've cleared a kitchen cupboard full of pots and pans, for example, scan the rest of the kitchen for any other similar cooking utensils that may be in another cupboard or the dishwasher and add them to the sort pile. If you've emptied a wardrobe, pull in any other garments from other areas of the home, such as the laundry pile, because to reduce your clothes down to a capsule collection you need to see everything that you own. Bring everything together in the largest clear space that you have – this could be over your bed, across a kitchen island, on the living room floor or (on a dry day) even out in the garden.

Kids' toys are the worst offenders when it comes to items that end up spread around the home. It's almost as though they come to life at night to make their way out of the toy box and into every conceivable space in the home. If you're trying to tackle the kids' toys, you're going to have to check everywhere – and we mean everywhere! – to be able to assess fully how many you have and to calculate how many you have space to keep. You do need to be able to see them all together to get to grips with the size of the problem. Only then can your kids decide which ones they love the most and want to keep.

Strip with purpose

The first stage, strip, is an important step in the *Sort Your Life Out* method as it's a way of gathering together everything relevant in the same space. It's your first opportunity to sift through all your possessions and take the initial step towards letting go of some things, if not physically, then emotionally. It's quite likely that while emptying a drawer or a cupboard, you'll come across certain possessions that you'd forgotten you even had. Just be aware that if you start reminiscing over old photographs or mementos, the stripping process will take that much longer. But if you come across something that is broken and beyond repair, you may want to recycle it straight away to get a headstart on the sorting process.

While you're stripping a space, work to a system rather than just randomly throwing a jumble of items into a single pile or box. The ideal way to strip any possessions is to gather all the similar items from one category together and arrange them in a group. Don't just shove all the family's shoes in one giant pile, instead make several smaller groupings and separate the kids' shoes into one zone and the adults' shoes into another zone. If you're gathering up all your clothes, keep all your winter coats and jackets in one section, cosy knitwear in another, then t-shirts and tops in another. You might choose to hang certain garments straight onto a temporary clothes hanging rail so that they're ready to sort once you've completed the assessment and cleaning of your space.

If you're stripping a space that contains lots of small items, self-sealing plastic bags are useful for keeping safe any tiny objects that could easily get lost, such as jewellery if it's not already stored in a box. Likewise, bag up any items that should be kept together and might otherwise get separated. Make sure you clearly label what is in each bag, especially if they're the nuts, bolts or other fixings for a particular piece of furniture.

TAKING IT ONE ROOM AT A TIME

If you have the space, stripping an entire room in one go is a step closer to how we approach the *Sort Your Life Out* method on the show. It's a good compromise between emptying a single cupboard and stripping the whole house. Breaking the task down and clearing one room at a time is the most practical approach for the majority of people, but as you clear each room make sure you still strip the space by the category of item. If you have items from one category in more than one space, like clothes or books, then try to gather them up from every corner and tackle that category in its entirety at the same time. Every time you tackle an entire category and sort through items added in from another room, you're making the job that much easier when you move on to the next room.

Once you've decided which room to tackle first, perhaps it's your bedroom, then gather up all the clothes, accessories and shoes from your wardrobe and drawers. If you're clearing the kitchen, empty every cupboard, drawer and shelf, then strip all the electrical appliances, kitchenware and perishable food items from the space. Scoop up every item from each category and gather them in one single space or box them all up for dealing with at the next stage. You need to gut the space to see it properly and understand its potential. When thinking about the best storage options for certain things, stay open-minded. Just because you've stored an item in a particular space in the past, that doesn't necessarily mean that's the ideal spot. It may well be that there is a better home for a certain object in another room, but sometimes you can only see that once the rooms are cleared and the items are grouped together.

THE FALL FAMILY, SERIES TWO

✳ 2,137 toys

✳ 452 books

✳ 13 guitars

✳ 61 mugs

✳ 1,274 tools

WHAT PERCENTAGE DO YOU NEED TO LOSE?

Whether you're emptying your entire home in one go or, for understandable practical reasons, you're tackling a smaller proportion of your space, it's really important to empty an entire cupboard or storage unit. Do not leave anything behind. Only by stripping a space entirely can you properly assess the amount of possessions you have, and what storage space you have to house it all, and therefore calculate the percentage of items that you need to lose. As a general rule, most families on the show need to discard fifty per cent of their things – yes, half their stuff – to double the space that they have to live in, but sometimes that creeps up to seventy per cent. In your home, some spaces may be more cluttered than others, so take it one step at a time. The cupboards in your kitchen might be bursting open, while your living room is perfectly under control, so take a realistic view of the area that you're tackling in that moment and decide how much you need to lose. If you don't clear everything out of a cupboard or drawer at the start and end up trying to clean and organise around a continuously moving pile of stuff that you haven't yet sorted, then you're far more likely to fail in your decluttering efforts.

Time to clean

If you have stripped an entire room of all your possessions, take the opportunity to give the room a thorough deep clean, including walls, windows, floors, units, shelves and surfaces. You can do this deep clean during any season – you don't have to wait until spring! Always deep clean the space before reintroducing any stuff, so that you're not trying to clean or tidy around piles of your possessions. And if you've stripped a single wardrobe of all your clothes, give that cupboard a proper clean while it's empty. When a space is looking sparkling clean, you can fully appreciate what you have, plus you'll feel less inclined to fill it back up with junk and more motivated to let go of lots of items.

 ## CLEANING KIT

There are endless cleaning products available to buy, each of them promising miracle results. But you don't need to spend a fortune on dozens of cleaners when a few all-purpose cleaners will do the job, and often a handful of cost-effective, common ingredients that you might already have in your kitchen cupboards will work just as well, and sometimes give even better results.

- ❏ MULTIPURPOSE SPRAY CLEANER

- ❏ DISINFECTANT SPRAY CLEANER

- ❏ BLEACH

- ❏ FURNITURE POLISH

- ❏ DISTILLED MALT VINEGAR
  (ALSO KNOWN AS WHITE VINEGAR)

- ❏ BICARBONATE OF SODA

- ❏ LEMON JUICE

- ❏ SALT

- ❏ SPRAY BOTTLE
  (FOR HOMEMADE CLEANING SOLUTIONS)

- ❏ MICROFIBRE CLOTHS

- ❏ OLD TOOTHBRUSHES

'THIS IS A PRIME EXAMPLE — YOU CAN HAVE ALL THE STORAGE IN THE WORLD, BUT IF YOU'VE GOT TOO MUCH STUFF TO FILL IT, THEN IT'S NOT GOING TO WORK FOR YOU!

STACEY

 THE DEEP-CLEANING BASICS FOR ANY ROOM

These are the basic steps to deep cleaning any room. You may need to add in a few extras, depending on what space you're tackling, but start here ...

✳ **Remove any cobwebs and dust from the ceiling and walls** – use a microfibre duster with a long handle or a microfibre cloth and a step ladder to clear any visible cobwebs and dust. Work from the ceiling and top of the walls downwards, starting with those hard-to-reach areas like high shelves, door frames and picture frames and working down to the coffee table and tops of skirting boards. If the dust situation is particularly bad, use a damp microfibre cloth. A great money-saving tip is to use an old sock pulled over your hand as a duster, which you can run over ledges, skirting and is especially good on slatted blinds or shutters. You can also use a vacuum cleaner to clear cobwebs. Follow Iwan's tip and attach a long cardboard poster tube to the vacuum cleaner nozzle to effortlessly reach high ceilings. Because the tube is only cardboard, it doesn't scrape or scratch any paintwork. And to access any awkward spaces, you can squeeze the end of the tube to make a handy nozzle shape.

✳ **Clean any light fittings** – they quickly gather dust, so wipe them thoroughly with a cloth both on the outside and inside.

✳ **Clean any shutters or blinds** – any window coverings that have slats will gather dust, but you can clean them in situ with a handheld vacuum cleaner and a microfibre cloth. Close the shutter or blind and clean the slats in one direction, then close them in the opposite direction and do the same again.

✳ **Clean any radiators** – most of us have radiators throughout our home but if they are very dusty, then they lose their efficiency in circulating heat. Use a long, thin microfibre radiator brush (which looks a bit like Marge Simpson's hair) to get in between the convector fins.

✳ **Wipe down all surfaces** – use a multipurpose spray cleaner and a damp microfibre cloth to remove any dust and wipe clean every surface, including shelves, units, drawers and tables.

✳ **Disinfect any handles and switches** – because door handles, light switches and the areas around them are touched most often, they're prone to getting dirty and oily. For that reason, it's a good idea to use a disinfectant spray cleaner on these areas. Remember to run your cloth over all the skirting boards around the room, as this is somewhere that dust accumulates.

TIP ✳
CLEAN FROM THE TOP DOWN

Always clean a room from the top down, so if you dislodge any dust and dirt that then settles, you won't need to clean it up twice.

✳ **Clean all windows and mirrors** – using a microfibre cloth and a spray bottle filled with equal parts of distilled malt vinegar and water, wipe away any smudges or streaks from windows and mirrors.

✳ **Vacuum the carpet, cupboards, drawers and other spaces** – run the vacuum cleaner over the floor, paying particular attention to where the floor meets the skirting board. Move any furniture out of the way to pick up any dust bunnies that have gathered beneath. You can even vacuum inside cupboards and drawers, if necessary.

✳ **Sweep and mop any hard floors** – brush up any dust and debris before mopping the floor with a well-wrung-out floor mop, then leave it to dry. If there is an excessive amount of dust, wet the rubber gloves on your hands and scrape up the dust from the floor. Any dust and pet hair will stick to the gloves, which can then be rinsed off.

✳ **Congratulate everyone on a job well done and celebrate your dazzlingly clean space with a cup of tea and a slice of cake.**

TIPS ✳

UNCRUSH YOUR CARPET

If your carpet has been indented by furniture, pop an ice cube onto the crushed carpet fibres and leave it to melt. As the ice melts, the carpet fibres will swell and regain their shape. If you need to, fluff up the fibres even further with a teaspoon.

UNSTICK YOUR HOUSE

To remove any sticky residue left on furniture, such as from kids' stickers, warm the area using a hairdryer to make it easier to scrape off. Alternatively, you can buy a special removal spray that when applied to the area melts the residue away.

KEEP MOTHS AT BAY

Clothes moths love to feast on natural fabrics stored in dark places, so your wardrobe and drawers are basically a buffet for them. Bay leaves are a natural deterrent, so to keep moths at bay, simply pop a few leaves into each clean drawer before returning your clothes.

HOW TO DEEP CLEAN A BEDROOM

Everyone deserves their bedroom to be a clean and serene sanctuary. In fact, the bedroom is one of the easiest spaces in the home to clean. Follow the deep cleaning basics above, with the following extras …

* **Strip the bed** – if you haven't already removed the bed linen, duvet, pillows and mattress cover as part of the stripping and packing stage, remove everything from the bed and launder all the items following the care instructions.

* **Freshen up the mattress** – vacuum the mattress and then sprinkle bicarbonate of soda over the entire surface. Leave it for an hour to allow any smells and moisture to be absorbed. Vacuum the mattress again, then rotate and turn it over. Ideally, this should be done every 6 to 12 months.

* **Remove any make-up stains** – If any surface is stained by make-up, use a little make-up remover on a cotton pad.

HOW TO DEEP CLEAN A BATHROOM

It's essential to keep the bathroom spotlessly clean, because … well, we all know what happens in there. On top of your regular cleaning routine, it's good to give everything a deep clean from time to time.

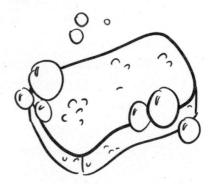

✳ **Clean the showerhead** – to clean a clogged-up showerhead, place the showerhead into a plastic bag and then fill the bag with distilled malt vinegar, a cola drink or a limescale cleaner until the showerhead is completely submerged. Tape the bag closed tightly around the connecting hose to the showerhead. The liquid is acidic and so it gets to work on any limescale. Leave it for a few hours or overnight before rubbing over the showerhead with a brush or cloth and rinsing away the liquid.

✳ **Clean the bathtub and shower door** – make a thick paste by mixing together one cup of bicarbonate of soda with a few teaspoons of distilled malt vinegar. Apply the paste to the surface of the tub or door – if it's thick enough it will stay in place. Leave it for an hour before rubbing with a microfibre cloth and then rinsing.

✳ **Clean the tile grout and sealant around the bathtub** – dip an old toothbrush in neat bleach and use it to scrub the grout between tiles. For the sealant around the bathtub, run a line of neat bleach along the sealant and hold it in place with cotton wool balls until the sealant returns to its original white colour.

✳ **Clean the ceiling, walls and surfaces** – spray all the surfaces with a multipurpose spray cleaner then, with the window and door closed, create lots of steam by turning on the shower and running some very hot water for five minutes. Turn the shower off and leave the bathroom, closing the door behind you. Leave the steam and cleaner to do their work for 30 minutes. After the steam bath, wipe down all the surfaces with a dry microfibre cloth.

✳ **Clean the toilet** – if limescale has built up in your toilet, remove as much water as you can from the bowl and then pour in plenty of distilled malt vinegar. Wear protective goggles and gloves and watch out for any splashes as you don't want to smell like a chip shop. Do not flush the toilet for at least three hours. If there is still some limescale left after this time, use a sheet of medium sandpaper to dislodge any last bits. You can also buy a set of loo brushes that are adapted to fit onto a power drill. Once any limescale has been removed, whizz round the bowl with toilet cleaner and then attack it with the power drill-loo brush, getting right up around the rim. Learn from Iwan's mistake: don't wear white jeans when attempting this. Finally, use a disinfectant spray on the toilet flush handle.

✳ **Clean the sink** – make a paste from bicarbonate of soda, lemon juice and some salt, then use this to scrub the basin. It smells so good. For any limescale around the taps, soak a cloth in distilled malt vinegar, wrap the cloth around the tap where the limescale is and leave in place for 15 minutes. Follow up by attacking the limescale with a toothbrush.

✳ **Clean all windows and mirrors** – follow the basic instructions on page 59, but whenever you clean a bathroom mirror, finish by putting a layer of car wax over the surface. This will stop the mirror steaming up whenever you take a shower or bath.

TIPS ✳

TOOTHPASTE TAPS

If you drop a blob of toothpaste into the basin when brushing your teeth, don't just rinse it down the plughole. Use it to clean around the taps using an old toothbrush before removing it with a damp cloth. The abrasive action of the toothpaste makes it a good gentle cleaner and brings the taps up to a good shine.

TOILET BOMBS

Toilet bombs make a loo lovely and fragrant, plus they give the boys something to aim at. To make your own, mix one cup of bicarbonate of soda and half a cup of citric acid with essential oils, such as mint, orange or lemon. Pack the mixture tightly into silicone moulds and leave to set at room temperature. Store them in a Kilner jar and pop one into the toilet bowl whenever you want to freshen up the loo.

DON'T FORGET YOUR TOOTHBRUSH!

For once, don't throw away old toothbrushes when they're worn out and being replaced. Keep them as essential cleaning tools that are excellent for getting right into awkward places. Just make sure that you do not mix them up in the bathroom.

HOW TO DEEP CLEAN A KITCHEN

As the hub of the home and the space where we prepare our food, the kitchen must be kept hygienic at all times. A deep clean doesn't have to take hours, especially when you have a regular cleaning routine in place.

* **Wipe down the ceilings and walls** – in the kitchen, the ceiling and walls are more likely to need a thorough wipe down because of the splashes that occur during cooking. Don't forget the tops of units and the fridge, which get quickly coated in a sticky film of grease and dust.

* **Deep clean the dishwasher** – place a dishwasher-safe bowl filled with a cup of distilled malt vinegar on the top rack of your dishwasher and run the hottest cycle, or you can use a special dishwasher cleaner and run the cleaning cycle. This deep clean should ideally be done once a month.

* **Deep clean the freezer and fridge** – fill your spray bottle with equal parts distilled malt vinegar and hot water. Unplug the freezer or fridge and remove any food. Take out any removable drawers and shelves. Working from the top downwards, generously spritz the inside with the vinegar spray, then wipe the cleaner away with a dry microfibre cloth. To remove any food spillages, scrub them clean with an old toothbrush dipped in hot water or using an abrasive paste made of bicarbonate of soda and a drop of washing-up liquid. Wash any removable drawers and shelves in warm soapy water, then dry them thoroughly.

✳ **Deep clean the oven** – remove the trays and racks from the oven. Scrape any fat straight into the bin to avoid blocking the sink or drain. To degrease the trays, place a dishwasher tablet in the trays and pour over boiling water. Leave this to work its magic, as the dishwasher tablet will break down the fat. Meanwhile, unclip the glass panel from the oven door. You can clean the glass door with a scraper or you can use another dishwasher tablet to scrub away grime. Scrape up any baked-on gunk from the bottom of the oven. Once it's clean, add a reusable oven liner to the bottom of the oven to make the task much easier next time.

✳ **Clean the microwave** – fill a microwaveable bowl with water and add a lemon cut in half. Heat the water in the microwave to create lemon-scented steam and leave it for 15 minutes while it takes a sauna. Whip around with a dry cloth afterwards. Ideally, give your microwave a steam clean every week.

✳ **Clean the sink drain hole** – unscrew the drain hole cover using a radiator key, then clean all around the plughole to prevent blockages. Use a toothbrush to really get in there.

✳ **Wipe down any small appliances** – unplug the appliance and tip or brush away any crumbs and food particles. If the appliance has any removable parts that can be put into the dishwasher, clean those separately. Wipe over the appliance with a damp microfibre cloth and a disinfectant spray, paying particular attention to the control panel, buttons or handle. If the appliance has a non-stick surface, like a toastie maker, never use a harsh scrubbing pad or sharp tool.

✳ **Clean and disinfect the kitchen bin** – take out the rubbish bag and mop up any smelly bin juices swilling around the bottom of the bin. Generously spritz the inside of the bin with a disinfectant spray. If it's really dirty, you may need to scrub it with a brush. A plastic bin can be cleaned on the outside with the same disinfectant spray, but a stainless-steel bin is best cleaned on the outside with a damp microfibre cloth.

TIPS ✳

DESCALE THE COFFEE MACHINE

To descale a coffee machine, pour some distilled malt vinegar into the reservoir and top it up with cold water. Run the cleaning cycle on the coffee machine, then once it's reached the end of that cycle, rinse out the reservoir. Always check the manufacturer's instructions that come with the gadget.

MAKE YOUR OWN CLEANING PADS

For cost-effective cleaning, take one of those small net bags that are used by supermarkets as packaging for fruit, onions and garlic. Scrunch up that net bag and use it with a paste made from bicarbonate of soda for some extra abrasive power. Using something that you would ordinarily just throw away is a total win.

HOW TO DEEP CLEAN THE LIVING ROOM

With a lot of daily traffic, the living room is probably the busiest room in the home. As this space is where the entire family spends most of its time, things can get messy and dirty pretty quickly. Give the space a satisfyingly deep clean by following this plan ...

* **Polish wooden furniture** – use a spray polish and a soft cloth to clean wooden furniture of regular dust. If the wood is dry and needs feeding, then consider using a furniture wax or oil, following the manufacturer's instructions. If there are any marks such as crayon on a tabletop, give the wood a light sanding before applying a coat of tung oil, which is food-safe and doesn't discolour. For any biro marks, hairspray can be really effective at removing those. Spritz on a little of the hairspray (it doesn't matter what hold!) and then, working fast, rub the area with a lightly coloured cloth. You should see a big improvement. Always do a patch test first, to make sure the hairspray will not damage the colour or stain on wood.

* **Reorganise the sofa** – straighten the seat and back cushions, fluff any extra cushions and fold any blankets or throws. If necessary, vacuum the upholstery to get rid of any pet hair, lint, dust or crumbs.

* **Clean the TV screen** – screens are a magnet for dust, so gently wipe them up and down with a dry microfibre cloth. You can use a slightly damp cloth to tackle any stains but never spray water or cleaner directly onto a screen.

||| HOW TO DEEP CLEAN A UTILITY ROOM

❋ **Deep clean the washing machine drawers and filter** – if your machine starts to smell, it could be due to a build-up of gunk in the detergent drawer. Remove the drawer, which should pull out, and then clean both the drawer and the cavity. Sprinkle some bicarbonate of soda into the cavity then, using your hand, rub it all around. Spritz on plenty of distilled malt vinegar from a spray bottle and leave the mixture to fizz up before wiping it away and replacing the clean drawer. Next, tackle the filter. Lay a towel down beneath the filter door to catch any liquid that escapes, then unscrew the filter and give it a good wipe over. People often find missing items while doing this, from pound coins to guitar picks. Ideally, you should deep clean your washing machine at least four times a year, depending on usage.

❋ **Deep clean the tumble dryer** – remove as much lint and fluff from the filter as you can, using a bendy brush to get into the tricky corners. You can use the vacuum nozzle to get it really clean. It's good to clean the filter regularly (ideally every few months, but more often if you have pets) because it keeps your dryer running efficiently and reduces the risk of any fires. Wipe the inside of the drum and door seal with a microfibre cloth dampened with your distilled malt vinegar spray. The same cloth can be used to wipe down the exterior of the tumble dryer too.

✳ **Vacuum any rugs and carpet** – for any that are relatively clean, a thorough vacuuming should be enough. But if the floor covering is lightly soiled, consider hiring a carpet cleaner. It's best to work in sections using straight strokes that slightly overlap (like mowing a lawn), so you can keep track of where you've cleaned. A woollen rug can be given a bath in warm water. Run the bath and add some bicarbonate of soda, a washing detergent pod and a dash of fabric softener, then dunk the rug in the bath until it's immersed and leave to soak.

The benefits of a clean home can be felt as well as seen. When everything is sparklingly clean and fresh, we can be calmer and more content, and you can feel a sense of pride in where you live too. If you can make the cleaning process fun, then household chores won't feel, well, like so much of a chore. Stick on a favourite song, pull on your dusting slippers and get moving. You could even make it part of family time, with one person dusting while someone else follows along with the vacuum. Remember, most cleaning tasks only take ten minutes or less and with everyone pulling together, it will be done in a flash.

TIPS ✳

CLEAN YOUR LOG BURNER

If you have a log burner with a window, use some of the ash from inside to clean the door. Pick up a tiny bit of fine ash on a damp cloth and then work it over the glass in circles. Only do this when the log burner is cool and use fine ash to avoid scratching the glass.

REMOVE PAINT FROM A LEATHER SOFA

To remove spilt paint from a leather sofa, use the blade of a knife with a little olive oil to stop it from scratching the leather. Afterwards, work the leather with a shoe polish containing wax for a shiny finish.

BANANA CLEANING YOUR PLANTS

Clean the leaves of a house plant with the inside of banana skins. The leaves absorb the potassium and are left looking shiny and healthy.

ECO—FRIENDLY WIPES

Single-use cleaning wipes are expensive and wasteful, but you can make your own eco-friendly version using reusable bamboo wipes that can be bought online. Mix equal parts water and distilled malt vinegar with a squirt of washing-up liquid. You can add a few drops of lemon juice, too. Add the bamboo wipes to the liquid and pre-soak them before using. The bamboo wipes can be washed and reused up to 120 times before discarding.

'A CLEAN SPACE IS A CALM SPACE.'

IWAN

Step One: Strip Checklist

1. SELECT THE SPACE YOU PLAN TO DECLUTTER.

2. REMOVE EVERYTHING FROM THAT SPACE, LEAVING NOTHING BEHIND.

3. GATHER ALL THE ITEMS READY TO SORT, GROUPING ALL THE SIMILAR THINGS.

4. DEEP CLEAN THE SPACE WHILE IT'S EMPTY.

5. STAND BACK AND ADMIRE THE SPARKLINGLY CLEAN AND CLEAR SPACE — IT WILL LOOK SO NICE THAT HOPEFULLY YOU'LL FEEL MOTIVATED NOT TO FILL IT BACK UP AGAIN WITH ALL THAT UNNECESSARY CLUTTER!

Congratulations! Your family has just completed step one and taken that all-important first step towards a fresh new start. If the amount of stuff you've just stripped from a space seems an impossible mountain to climb, just remember that this is the worst it will ever be. Things will only improve from here on. Plus, as a family, you've got your support team around you and together you can tackle anything. You've got this.

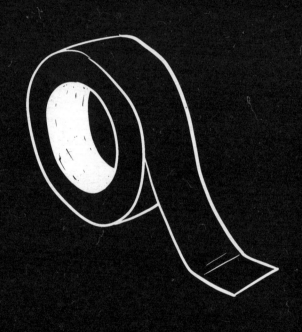

STEP TWO

SORT

The second stage of the *Sort Your Life Out* method is to sort through all your possessions. This is your family's opportunity to put behind them any previous habits that have led anyone to cling on to too much stuff and look forward to a clean slate. This is your chance to declutter and, in doing so, to reconnect with your possessions, to remind yourself what you love, why you love it and why you want to have it in your home.

Once you've emptied out the drawer, cupboard or room, gathered together your possessions, grouped them by category and cleaned the space, you can then move on to sorting your stuff. Find the largest space that you have to work in. This could be the living room floor with all the furniture pushed back and everything cleared out the way, or on a fine day it could be a space in the garden where you can work in the open air. Either way, lay down a dust sheet to give yourself a clean surface to work on and then lay out all the items in each category ready to sort.

THE VINEY FAMILY, SERIES TWO

* 532 plastic carrier bags

* Over 205 hair rollers

* 30 umbrellas

* 18 unused toothbrushes

* 17 old digital cameras

* 443 pairs of shoes (half of which had never been worn)

'IF YOUR HOUSE IS FULL OF CLUTTER AND YOU DON'T KNOW WHERE TO START, FIND ONE TINY SPACE, FOCUS ON THAT, REMOVE EVERYTHING FROM THAT SPACE AND THEN PUT BACK ONLY WHAT YOU NEED, USE OR LOVE. IT WORKS.'

STACEY

Divide to conquer

No matter what space you've stripped, when sorting through your possessions you need to follow our *Sort Your Life Out* method and arrange all the items by category. If you've already grouped the items when unpacking the drawer or cupboard you should have a head start on this, but as a reminder, the categories are:

- ❑ CLOTHES, ACCESSORIES AND SHOES
- ❑ TOILETRIES, MAKE—UP AND SCENTS
- ❑ KITCHENWARE
- ❑ PERISHABLE FOOD ITEMS
- ❑ CLEANING PRODUCTS
- ❑ TOWELS, BED LINENS AND BLANKETS
- ❑ BOOKS
- ❑ ELECTRONICS DEVICES, DVDS AND/OR CDS
- ❑ PAPERWORK
- ❑ CHILDREN'S TOYS

- [ ] LEISURE ITEMS
- [ ] PHOTOGRAPHS
- [ ] SENTIMENTAL OBJECTS

Each of these categories is fairly broad, however, and so it's necessary to drill down even further and subdivide these main categories to streamline the sorting process. Taking books as an example, you might want to separate all your books into genres, so into fiction and non-fiction, with subcategories for cookery books, travel guides and so on. For clothes, you'll need to separate out those belonging to each family member and then group them so that all the coats and jackets are together, all the knitwear is together, working down to t-shirts, vests and underwear.

MARK OUT YOUR SPACE

In the warehouse, we mark out the floorspace with yellow lines to clearly show where one category ends and another starts, and then we group all the similar items together. If it's helpful to you to do the same, then mark out areas on the floor with strips of masking tape to help keep things organised as you sort. It's always useful to label things in order to keep track, so you may want to outline a bit of floor space as 'Rex's toys' and another bit as 'Rose's toys', for example, so that things don't become a confusing jumble. If you're able to borrow a couple of hanging rails for clothes (see page 134), they're really handy to have.

||| KEEP, SELL, DONATE OR RECYCLE

During the sorting process, you'll decide what to do with each item based on the following four options:

- ☐ KEEP
- ☐ SELL
- ☐ DONATE
- ☐ RECYCLE

While you're sorting, it's sensible to leave all the 'keep' items in situ on the floor. With everything laid out, you can clearly see what you're holding on to and you might just revisit some of your 'keep' decisions later on in the sorting process to let more go, which is easier to do when items are still laid out and not jumbled up in a pile or stashed in boxes. On the show, we create three giant piles of possessions to sell, donate and recycle, so that the family can see just how much they've managed to let go of. It can provide the much-needed motivation to keep going. Feel free to do the same if you think it will help you to power through. But if you're restricted with space or you'd rather tidy stuff away as you sort, have a cardboard box or reusable shopping bag each for 'sell', 'donate' and 'recycle' and pop things straight into the appropriate box once you've decided how best to move it on. If you're the kind of person who is likely to backtrack on decisions and pull things out of piles, then this out-of-sight-out-of-mind approach may be a better option for you. Either way, as you'll be paying a visit to your local car boot sale, charity shop and recycling centre, it's useful to have some spare cardboard boxes and strong bags for transporting all the things that you decide not to keep.

||| EASE YOURSELF IN

On the show, when we're helping a family sort through their stuff in the warehouse, initially it can be completely overwhelming for them. To ease people into the process of saying goodbye to their things, it's a really good idea to start with a category of possessions that ordinarily don't have a lot of sentimental meaning attached to them. No one can really feel that emotionally connected to fifty-one odd socks or thirty-four pots of nail varnish and so it's often these kinds of items that are a good entry point.

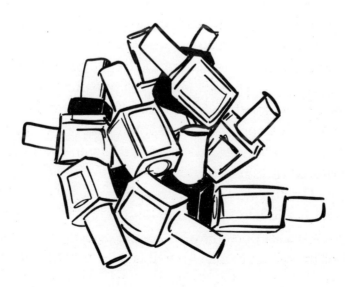

Do the same at home and ease yourself in gently with a category that you feel you can make swift decisions over – for some families this might be clothes, for others it might be kitchen utensils. In this book, we're going to start with the bedroom and make clothes the first category that we apply. the *Sort Your Life Out* method to. With clothes, they might be worn and tatty, no longer suit your style or no longer fit, so there should be some straightforward decisions to be made there. Then you can move on to the bathroom and toiletries and beauty products. Some of these might be half empty, dried out or duplicates that you'll never get through before they pass their use-by date, so again, some clear-cut choices can be made there.

If you feel that you're going to struggle emotionally when it comes to items like photographs, souvenirs, mementos and even kids' toys, then leave those categories until last. By that point, hopefully, you'll be in the letting-go groove and already be feeling the benefits of releasing yourself from unnecessary clutter.

THE SMITH FAMILY, SERIES TWO

* 207 loose nappies

* 24 used toothbrushes

* 145 Punjabi suits

* 1 year subscription of *Men's Health* magazines unopened

'WHEN YOU'VE GOT AN ABUNDANCE OF STUFF AND ALL OF THOSE ITEMS HOLD EMOTIONAL ATTACHMENTS, START WITH THE LESS OVERWHELMING STUFF AND THEN WORK YOUR WAY UP TO THE THINGS THAT REALLY HOLD YOU BACK EMOTIONALLY. THEY ARE A PART OF US AND IT'S HARD TO LET GO SOMETIMES.'

STACEY

Do the maths

By now you'll have already cleared your space and thoroughly cleaned it, so you'll have got an accurate idea of what proportion of your stuff you can comfortably store. Let's say that you've gathered up all your cookbooks, dusted the bookshelf and have calculated that the shelf can hold 25 books, then that's your target. The percentage of how much of your stuff you need to let go of depends entirely on your starting point, but whether you've got 30, 50 or over 100 (it has been known) books to begin with, always remember **the golden rule:** never keep more than you can store.

||| FOCUS ON YOUR GOAL

Once you've set the target number for what to keep based on the space you have, maintain focus on that goal. Think of it as choosing your top favourites in that category. Concentrating on the best or best-loved items that will make you happy is often easier than dwelling on the items that you need to let go of. So, set a number, stick to it and opt to keep only those items that add value to your daily life.

⫼ QUESTION EACH ITEM

This is when you need to get a little ruthless and start to pare back your possessions. There are some basic key questions while you are in the midst of the sort process. These questions can vary depending on the room and category of items you're sorting, but continually ask yourself:

☐ DO I NEED IT?

☐ DO I USE IT?

☐ DO I LOVE IT?

⫼ COMPARE AND DISCARD

Making the sometimes-tricky decision over what to keep and what to discard is usually made easier by comparing similar items. Rather than simply picking up item A and asking yourself, 'Do I want to keep this? Or can I let it go?' try comparing item A with item B or item C and then choosing your favourite from the options. When forced to make a decision between this or that, you'll generally be able to express a preference and there'll be a clear winner.

'WHY ARE YOU KEEPING THINGS IN YOUR HOME THAT YOU DON'T LOVE OR YOU DON'T NEED? YOU'RE SURROUNDING YOURSELF WITH NEGATIVE ENERGY. KEEP THE THINGS THAT MAKE YOU HAPPY. KEEP THE THINGS THAT ARE PURPOSEFUL. ANYTHING ELSE, LET IT GO!'

DILLY

KEEP PUSHING FORWARD

Try to make decisions quickly and keep moving on. If you hesitate over an item, put it back down and go back to it at the end after you've sorted through the rest of the things in that category, so it doesn't distract you and interrupt your flow. By the time you've reviewed the other things in that category, on the second pass, you may feel more decisive about the item you initially hesitated over. You need to avoid wavering, losing interest and quitting halfway through.

 NEVER SAY 'MAYBE'

Avoid having a 'maybe' pile. If anything is a 'maybe', then you're clearly not passionate about it and it isn't something to keep. Saying 'maybe' is simply a way of putting off making a decision, so stop dithering and add it to your sell, donate or recycle pile.

THE FARROW FAMILY, SERIES THREE

* 32 rolls of wallpaper

* 81 satchels and handbags

* 241 balls of wool

* 92 chopping boards

* 116 different cleaning products

KEEP YOUR REASON WHY IN MIND

Whenever you feel like you're flagging or clinging on to too much stuff, remind yourself of the reason why you're doing this (see page 18). Taking a moment to reconnect with the 'why' and not the 'how' should give you a renewed energy to crack on.

REAL LIFE INSPO

In series one, when Taurean was really struggling with letting go of his first-ever computer even though it no longer turned on, we took a moment to consider the reason why the family was going through this process, which was his wife's health and well-being. Following an accident, Kirsty was left with reduced mobility and could easily trip over any clutter left lying around the home. The very powerful 'why' for Taurean and the rest of the family was peace of mind knowing that Kirsty would be safe and Kirsty herself regaining her independence.

'WE'RE NOT LIVING OUR BEST LIVES. I'M READY FOR A CLEAN SLATE.'

VENICIA, SERIES THREE

Follow up on your decisions

Once you've committed to let something go, do it. If you've decided to sell certain possessions, get on and list them online or do that car boot sale. Why not book a slot at your local car boot sale in advance? That way you've got a deadline to motivate you to work towards. If you're donating items, then arrange delivery or collection with your chosen charity. And if you're recycling goods, make the necessary arrangements to recycle them in the most appropriate way. Never, ever move piles of items from one space to another, so you're just pushing the problem on. The objective is to let go and clear space, rather than tidy up one area by moving the clutter into another part of your home. Always finish the sorting and letting go process before moving on to systemising and organising. You only want to be dedicating space to those possessions that you have committed to keeping. If you don't discard everything else, then it will all creep back in and, before you know it, your home will be clutter-central once more.

THE LESPEARE FAMILY, SERIES ONE

* 4 toastie makers

* 36 shower gels

* 18 gaming controllers

* 84 bottles of condiments

'THE MOST ANNOYING THING WAS THE CHARITY BAGS. WE GOT RID OF ALL THE CLOTHES, WE PUT THEM ALL IN CHARITY BAGS, BUT THEN WE NEVER ACTUALLY TOOK THEM TO A CHARITY SHOP.'

AEVERI, SERIES ONE

Sorting room by room

 SORT > THE MASTER BEDROOM

Clothes, accessories and shoes

As you've already stripped the space and cleaned everything thoroughly, you can take a moment to assess the storage and calculate how much space you have and therefore how much stuff you can realistically reintroduce to the room. The main items to sort in the bedroom are clothes, accessories and shoes. As you can only keep the amount of clothes that you can comfortably store, while sorting set aside to keep only what you wear, what you need, what you love and what you fit. Ask yourself the following questions:

- ❑ DO I WEAR IT OFTEN?

- ❑ WILL I WEAR IT AGAIN?

- ❑ DOES IT MAKE ME FEEL GOOD?

- ❑ DOES IT FIT ME?

- ❑ DO I HAVE MULTIPLES?

- ❑ IS IT IN WEARABLE CONDITION?

If you have or can borrow a freestanding hanging rail, line up all your clothes on hangers so that you can see clearly what you have – this makes the sorting process so much easier. And if you're sorting more than one person's clothes, then it's a bonus if each person can have their own rail.

GO SHOPPING IN YOUR OWN WARDROBE

Everyone has claimed at times that they've got absolutely nothing to wear, and yet the wardrobe doesn't close because it's brimming with clothes. Why? Because over time we become too familiar with all those clothes that we already own and the thrill of any new garment quickly wears off after purchase. The more clothes we accumulate and the trickier they are to store and find, the more likely we are to forget what we have. So, go shopping in your own wardrobe rather than on the high street. You'll rediscover garments that you'd forgotten all about and it'll feel like you've got brand new pieces to wear. But when you do go shopping in your own wardrobe, remember the mantra when sorting clothes: only keep what you wear, what you need, what you love and what you fit.

CREATE A CAPSULE WARDROBE

The ideal is to create a capsule collection that is classic, flexible and can be combined in many different ways. Build a wardrobe of hardworking basics that you really love. When you buy something, think about how many other pieces in your wardrobe it will go with – aim for a maximum number of outfits from the minimum number of pieces. An easy way to ensure that everything goes together is to stick to a palette of complementary colours in that look good together.

REPAIR, REPURPOSE OR RECYCLE

Sometimes the condition of a garment means it's only fit for recycling, no matter how much you love it. If anything has a hole but is otherwise in a wearable condition, consider whether it can be repaired with invisible darning or perhaps even visible mending, including patches and embroidery stitches. If not, ask yourself if the garment can be repurposed. Odd socks can make useful cleaning cloths and an old dressing gown can be cut up to make handy dusters.

Depending on how much cupboard space you have elsewhere, you may also house towels, bed linens and blankets in a bedroom, but for the purposes of this book, we discuss all these in the utility room section on page 184.

SORT > THE KIDS' BEDROOMS

Clothes, accessories and shoes

Apply the same principles to your kids' wardrobes as to your own adult clothes. The difference here is that they're far more likely to have outgrown something in what feels like record time. The good news is that there will be other parents and guardians who'll be incredibly grateful for what you no longer need. In fact, there are even charity shops that are dedicated entirely to kids' stuff.

KIDS SHOES

Choose one pair each of trainers, smart shoes, school shoes and seasonal shoes (summer sandals or winter boots), so in total you only need to keep a maximum of five pairs per child.

'I'M PROUD OF US. I KEEP IN THE BACK OF MY MIND HOW WE STARTED OUT AND HOW HARD IT WAS FINANCIALLY, SO IT'S NICE THAT WE'VE COME ACROSS A LOT OF KIDS' STUFF THAT'S STILL IN GOOD CONDITION AND THAT WE CAN PASS ON TO OTHERS.'

DAN, SERIES TWO

SORT > THE BATHROOM

Toiletries, make-up and scents

The bathroom is one of the quickest spaces to strip and sort, so it feels like an easy win. To whittle down your bathroom products to those essentials that form your core daily routine, ask yourself these following questions:

☐ DO I USE IT OFTEN?

☐ WILL I USE IT AGAIN?

☐ DOES IT MAKE ME FEEL GOOD?

☐ DO I HAVE DUPLICATES?

☐ IS IT OVER 12 MONTHS OLD?

☐ IS IT EMPTY, DRIED OUT, DISCOLOURED OR SMELLS FUNNY?

CHECK THE DATE

Immediately get rid of anything empty or almost empty, or that looks or smells funny. Toiletries and beauty products have a relatively short shelf life, so discard anything that's been hanging around for a while. Make-up has a particularly short shelf life before it goes off, so it's unwise to hold on to any product for more than 12 months. Out-of-date make-up can be a cause of infection, especially around the eyes. Likewise, aftershave and perfume go off and the scent changes over time. This can happen quite rapidly if the bottle is left in sunlight, making it smell bitter when past its best.

MOVE ON ANY MULTIPLES

If you've got unopened duplicates of any products and you know that you're not going to get through them before they're likely to go off, then move them on now by donating them to a hygiene bank or giving them to family, friends or neighbours. Commit to using up what you already have before buying more, otherwise they'll go out of date too.

STREAMLINE TO SAVE TIME

Streamline your bathroom products to reflect your daily routine. Most of us only really ever use the essentials each day – shampoo, conditioner, shower gel, cleanser, moisturiser, deodorant, toothpaste – so keep one of each of those, plus an in-date back-up if you must.

TIP ✳
MAKE–UP MAKE–BELIEVE

Kids love to copy their parents and older siblings, so if you have a little one in the household who is fascinated by make-up, you could always make them their own mini make-up bag with a few in-date duplicates. When we organised the Harris-Hawley home in series two, to save teenager Mia's favourite beauty products, we popped a few little bits of make-up that she didn't want to keep for herself into a special case for her much younger sister Cece to play with whenever Mia was getting ready.

SORT > THE KITCHEN

Kitchenware, perishable food items and cleaning products

As the heart of the home, kitchens can quickly become a dumping ground for random items – paperwork, toys, devices – with cluttered countertops. This is a room where lots of small items are usually stored, so this is one of the biggest tasks in the home. Set aside a good amount of time to work through it all and always keep the core purpose of the space as your focus when sorting through your kitchen stuff. So that you know exactly how much of everything you have, group kitchen items together in these subcategories:

* Appliances

* Cooking utensils

* Crockery, cutlery and glassware

* Storage containers

* Perishable food items

* Cleaning products

APPLIANCES

Be realistic when assessing how frequently you use something. Does that ice cream maker sit in its box for 11 months of the year? Do you need it at all when you could make no-churn ice cream the one or two times in the summer you actually get round to making a batch? Similarly, does the bread maker/rice cooker/air fryer/sandwich toaster/coffee maker really earn the space that it takes up on the countertop?

COOKING UTENSILS

How many pots and pans you keep will depend entirely on how much you love to cook at home, but the average family doesn't really need more than three or four saucepans in different sizes. If you're really tight on space, there are now handy 'all-in-one' pans that are oven-safe too, so they do the job of lots of different pans in one.

CROCKERY, CUTLERY AND GLASSWARE

These don't necessarily need to be matching sets as gone are the days of a 32-piece dinner service in the same floral design. Your personal style might be to combine lots of slightly different colours or patterns. However, do be realistic as to how many of each item you need. Do you really need 12 of everything when there are just 2 of you in the house and your dining table only seats 6?

STORAGE CONTAINERS

We all end up with a stack of storage containers spilling out of the kitchen cupboards, especially as takeaway food often comes in plastic tubs. But only keep those that you actually have lids for, and not too many. Even if you batch cook for your family, only keep around ten containers with lids in different sizes for kitchen use – that should be enough. You could also repurposed extra containers that aren't being used for food – in series two, the Harris-Hawley family saved a lot of space by using their spares to store leftover paint, getting rid of their big half-empty paint tins.

'KITCHENS ARE A HOARDING GROUND. I BET IF ANYONE GOES TO THEIR CUPBOARD, THEY'VE GOT 40 OR 50 MUGS IN THERE THAT THEY DEFINITELY DON'T NEED. WHEN DO 40 PEOPLE EVER TURN UP AND ASK FOR A CUP OF TEA? IT JUST DOESN'T HAPPEN!'

STACEY

TIPS ✳

USE YOUR BEST EVERY DAY

Don't save things for best – when it comes to crockery, keep your very best set and start using it every day. What's the point in waiting until Christmas to get the good crockery out when you can make every day an occasion?

MAKE YOUR OWN ORGANISERS

If any storage containers have become separated from their lids, you don't need to throw them away. Use them as cost-effective organisers in other spaces, such as for make-up in the bathroom or for coloured plastic bricks in the kids' playroom.

PERISHABLE FOOD ITEMS

Deciding whether to keep or lose a food item should be a straightforward choice. Get rid of any out-of-date food immediately. Learn the difference between best-before dates and use-by dates. If things are past their use-by date, either throw them away or recycle them in your green food waste bin, then recycle packaging in the correct way. A best-before date is a guideline, rather than an absolute rule, so use your judgement. But even when something can still be used, if you're not going to consume that food item within the use-by timeframe, then move it on now. Donate any unopened tins or packets to a food bank by putting them in the donation bin at your local supermarket and for fresh produce, use a food-sharing app to rehome anything that is still edible but surplus to your requirements.

CLEANING PRODUCTS

We've already touched on the surprisingly small number of core cleaning products that you really need to clean your home (see page 55). You should already have a clear idea of what to keep as you've used them when you stripped and cleaned the space. Donate any surplus-to-requirements cleaning products to a local food bank that also tackles hygiene poverty.

 ## SORT > THE UTILITY ROOM

Towels, bed linens and blankets

If you're lucky enough to have one, you'll know that the utility room is another one of those spaces that can easily become cluttered. Don't lose sight of its true purpose.

TOWELS

Realistically you don't need that many towels per person: have one in use in the bathroom, one waiting to be used and one in the laundry, so that's three altogether per person. If you have pets, you may also want to keep one (separately) for them. Consider donating any unwanted towels to an animal charity or rehoming centre, which often need such items.

BED LINENS AND BLANKETS

The same rule applies to bed linens as for towels. You don't need more than three sets of linens per bed. If you prefer a duvet on your bed, you may not have any blankets at all, but sometimes it's nice to have a little extra warmth either when in bed or snuggled on the sofa. One per bed or one per person for snuggles should be plenty.

SORT > THE LIVING ROOM

Books, electronic devices, DVDs and CDs

A multipurpose space, the living room is an area used primarily for relaxation and entertainment. As well as those big items of furniture, like a sofa, armchairs and coffee table, the living room is somewhere that usually houses lots of small items too. Without adequate storage, piles of books, DVDs, CDs, magazines and papers can soon clutter the place up, so it's important to keep on top of these things by asking yourself, 'Do I need it? Do I use it? Do I love it?'

BOOKS

With the exception of kids' story books, reference books and cookbooks, most other books are 'single-use'. Once a novel has been read, the book is likely to then sit on a shelf without ever being looked at again. Unless you really love a novel and re-read it regularly, there's no need to hang on to any book that has served its purpose. This should be a category where you can gain some satisfying wins by easily losing plenty of books. Ask yourself these questions:

☐ HAVE I ALREADY READ IT?

☐ DO I REALLY LOVE IT?

☐ WILL I READ IT AGAIN?

☐ WILL I NEED TO REFER TO IT IN THE FUTURE?

TIPS ✳

GO DIGITAL

While there's nothing quite like turning a page to start the next chapter, there's no denying that printed books can take up a lot of physical space. If you're short on shelf space, then when you next go to buy a book consider an e-book that is read on a device that can contain hundreds of titles at once.

CLUB TOGETHER

Establish a book club with friends or neighbours so that you can pass around recommended reads. It's satisfying to know that someone else is making use of something that you're done with, plus you can chat about your thoughts on the book together the next time you catch up over a coffee.

DVDS AND CDS

This category should be the easiest win of all. Now we have streaming, there's far less need to hold on to movies or music in any physical format (unless you're a vintage vinyl collector, but that's another issue). Unless something is rare and might appeal to a collector, selling them on might be tricky as how many of us still have a DVD or CD player that we could actually play them on? And donating them to a charity shop may not be an option either as many now don't accept DVDs or CDs for the same reason – that there aren't many customers for these items nowadays. There are some websites that may buy DVDs and CDs for a small amount of money, but recycling is likely to be your best option here.

ELECTRONIC DEVICES

TVs, set-top boxes, mobiles, laptops, tablets, e-readers and games consoles are the most common electronics and devices that we now all seem to own. With tempting offers of regular upgrades, it's understandable that many of us seem to have a cupboard or drawer full of obsolete electronics, chargers and plugs that we haven't yet dealt with. If it's tucked away, then it's likely surplus to requirements, so ask yourself:

❏ DO I USE IT?

❏ DO I HAVE DUPLICATES?

❏ DOES IT WORK?

❏ DOES IT HAVE A RESALE VALUE?

TIP ✳
DIAL-A-DONATION

Even if a device no longer works, mobile phones and other electronics contain materials that can be recycled and so have a value to charity organisations. Certain charities will gladly accept a donation of your old mobiles when they're no longer of use to you. If any mobile does still work, reputable charities will wipe data from the device that you donate before reselling, but you can do it yourself by resetting the phone to factory settings.

SORT › THE KIDS' PLAY SPACE

Toys and books

Whether this is a separate room, a permanent area in another space or your living room doubles up as the kids' play space, it can frequently feel like there's been an explosion in a toy factory. In the homes of several families who we helped on the show, the number of kids' toys crept into the thousands. Interestingly, it wasn't the kids who struggled the most with letting go of their past toys, it was the parents. Setting any emotional attachment aside for now, consider the following:

- ❏ DOES MY CHILD PLAY WITH IT?

- ❏ DOES MY CHILD LOVE IT?

- ❏ IS IT AGE–APPROPRIATE?

- ❏ DO WE HAVE DUPLICATES?

LET YOUR CHILD DECIDE

As their parent or guardian, rather than imposing your choices on them, let your child choose what they love the most, play with and want to keep. You may be surprised at how their choices differ from what you expect.

DON'T WORRY ABOUT APPEARING RUDE

Letting go of toys when they've been given as gifts can feel disrespectful. It's understandable how you might worry that the person who gave it will think you've been rude in letting it go. But kids are given so many toys, especially in their early years, that it's unrealistic to expect them to hold on to every single one. Explain to the gift giver that your child has grown out of it and so you've donated it to a toy bank and now another child who doesn't have quite so much can enjoy it too. Hopefully, they'll understand and feel like the toy has been gifted for the second time.

TIP ✳
BATTERIES NOT INCLUDED

When recycling any kid's toy, take the battery pack out before depositing it at the recycling centre. Batteries can be recycled as well as the plastic toy, but this is best done separately.

||| SORT > THE WORKSPACE/HOME OFFICE

Paperwork

With the recent increase in homeworking, more and more of us need a dedicated workspace at home. Even if you don't need to do your day job from home, there's always a certain amount of paperwork attached to general house admin, from utility bills and guarantees for appliances to notes sent home from school. We all accumulate reams of paper throughout our adult lives. It seems to multiply and spread over every surface in every room of the home – the hall, the kitchen, the fridge door, the dining table, stuffed down the sides of the sofa … Rather than sort your paperwork into the usual four options, as paperwork has no inherent use or value to anyone else, we're going to deal with it slightly differently and assign everything to one of the following four options:

- ☐ ACTION
- ☐ FILE
- ☐ RECYCLE
- ☐ SHRED

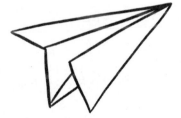

WORK TO A GRID SYSTEM

To make the sifting process easier, mark out a grid system on the floor and label each area with the relevant option – 'action', 'file', 'recycle' or 'shred'. This should enable you to speedily sort your pile of papers into more manageable piles that you can then deal with:

☐ ACTION – THINGS THAT YOU NEED TO ACT ON AS SOON AS POSSIBLE, SO THIS IS YOUR PILE OF PAPERWORK TO DEAL WITH NOW.

☐ FILE – THINGS THAT DO NOT NEED ANY ACTION, BUT THAT YOU MIGHT NEED TO REFER TO IN THE NEAR FUTURE (SUCH AS INSURANCE INFORMATION, TICKETS OR ALL THE ESSENTIAL DETAILS FOR THE SCHOOL TRIP COMING UP LATER ON IN THE YEAR).

☐ RECYCLE – THINGS THAT ARE NO LONGER RELEVANT OR NEEDED, BUT CONTAIN NO PERSONAL INFORMATION AND SO CAN BE PUT STRAIGHT INTO THE RECYCLING.

☐ SHRED – THINGS THAT ARE NO LONGER RELEVANT OR NEEDED, BUT THEY DO CONTAIN SENSITIVE INFORMATION SO THEY MUST BE SHREDDED FIRST AND THEN PUT INTO THE RECYCLING.

REAL LIFE INSPO

Many of us dread dealing with paperwork as it often has negative connotations, especially the letters that arrive in brown envelopes. In series three, we helped Tom tackle his home office where he had 130 unopened envelopes amongst a huge box of papers. The fact that some of it was confidential meant that he just put off dealing with it, even though he had a shredder.

Don't do a Tom and put off dealing with your papers as tackling it now will help you feel not just better organised physically but also mentally. And once you've dealt with both the recycle and shred-and-recycle piles, you'll be left with just the three piles to either action, file or archive (see more on page 199). Stay on top of things by regularly going through your files.

 SORT > SENTIMENTAL ITEMS

Photographs and objects

It's time to move on to what is potentially the trickiest category to sort through. By now you'll be well-practised in the art of letting go, but it's okay to stop and take a moment of reflection when it comes to those sentimental objects that mean something to you. Any type of object can be of huge sentimental importance to an individual, but it's not usually the object itself, it's what or who that object represents. Over the show, we've seen people emotionally attached to everything from their kids' babygrows and muslins to their sister's empty spice jars and dad's hammer. Only you know what items are significant to you and how you prefer to deal with them. Just remember that it's far better to have a few cherished items on display so that you can enjoy them every day than a trunk full of possessions that never see the light of day. Throwing the spotlight on those cherished possessions that you have deliberately decided to keep and allowing them

to shine is the best way to honour those memories. As for those items you decide to part with, do take some time with them – you may find it helps to enjoy that special something one last time with your family before letting go.

SORTING PHOTOGRAPHS

This is a category of items that is likely to bring up strong emotions because photographs take us right back to a time, place and people that we love and cherish. In order to enjoy them, photographs are best sorted into labelled albums or framed and displayed. But what if the memories that photographs bring back aren't straightforwardly happy ones because, well, the situation is complicated?

REAL LIFE INSPO

Divorced mum of three Steph, who we met in series one, had kept everything from her wedding in her loft. It was emotional for Steph to look through photographs, cards and even her wedding dress as they were all a reminder of happier, more optimistic times. Even though Steph had reached a place where she felt ready to let go of these memories, she selflessly took the decision to carefully store some wedding photographs in an album and other mementos in a sealed box in the loft so that they are there if any of her daughters ever wanted to share in those memories of their parents' marriage.

TIP *
TAKE THE EX TEST

When sorting any possession, test how much you really want to keep it by taking The Ex Test. Let's imagine that it was a messy break-up and you never want to see or speak to your ex ever again, but this particular possession is still at your ex's home. Ask yourself this: would you go through the agony and embarrassment of calling your ex to get it back? If you would, then you must really want the item. If you wouldn't, then it goes.

Step Two: Sort Checklist

---

1. LAY OUT ALL THE ITEMS IN THEIR CATEGORIES IN YOUR LARGEST WORKSPACE.

2. HAVE AN AREA, BOX OR BAG FOR THOSE SELL, DONATE AND RECYCLE ITEMS.

3. START WITH AN 'EASY' CATEGORY THAT HOLDS THE LEAST EMOTIONAL ATTACHMENT.

4. ASK YOURSELF, 'DO I NEED IT? DO I USE IT? DO I LOVE IT?'

5. STICK TO YOUR TARGET NUMBER OF ITEMS TO LET GO OF.

6. REMEMBER WHY YOU STARTED DOING THIS IN THE FIRST PLACE — WHETHER IT'S TO HAVE MORE TIME TO SPEND WITH THE FAMILY OR A BETTER QUALITY OF LIFE IN GENERAL — AND KEEP THAT LIFE-CHANGING GOAL IN MIND AT ALL TIMES.

Yay! We made it through step two. For many people, the sort stage can be really hard as it brings up lots of emotions that need to be worked through. But together you managed to let go of so many unnecessary or unwanted possessions. In fact, you all smashed it. Now you're putting back into your space only those things that you need or love, so the fun can really start ...

STEP THREE

SYSTEMISE

You've now all reached the third stage in the *Sort Your Life Out* method: systemise. This part of the process is the most important and the most fun. It's time to reap the benefit of all those tough decisions made during the sort stage. As your family's possessions are reintroduced to each space, you'll immediately see and feel the positive change brought about by clearing the clutter. If you've managed to cut your possessions by at least fifty per cent to make more space in your home, then there should be no more falling over trip-hazards, no more moving piles of junk to sit on the sofa, no more struggling to close cupboard doors. Because you can soon become blind to the everyday disaster zone that is a disorganised home, you may not have fully realised just how stressful daily life has become until you experience clutter-free bliss.

Now, if you were to put your whittled-down collection of possessions back into your home more or less where you stripped them from, your home would look great. But for how long ...? Without introducing proper systems, it's likely that old habits will creep back in along with a whole load more clutter and, before you know it, you'll be back where you started. The simple systems we suggest for each space are designed to make it easier for each home to be kept clean and tidy, for family life to run smoothly and to give everyone back more time in their day to do the things they love most.

Over the pages that follow, we tackle the house room by room and outline the systems to establish for an organised home. Boiled down to its essentials, during the systemising process you will:

- ❏ GIVE EVERY SPACE A CLEAR FUNCTION

- ❏ ORGANISE THE SPACE SO IT MAKES THE MOST SENSE

- ❏ MAXIMISE THE STORAGE POTENTIAL OF THE SPACE

- ❏ GIVE EVERY OBJECT A DESIGNATED SPACE

- ❏ LABEL ALL STORAGE SO OBJECTS ARE RETURNED TO THAT DESIGNATED SPACE

- ❏ MAKE SURE THE WHOLE FAMILY IS ON BOARD WITH THE NEW SYSTEMS, SO THEY'RE MAINTAINED GOING FORWARD

'THE CLEAN-UP EFFORT
USED TO BE A THREE-
OR FOUR-HOUR JOB,
BUT NOW WE CAN DO IT
IN TEN MINUTES BECAUSE
EVERYTHING HAS A HOME.
AND WE CAN SPEND
OUR EVENINGS HAVING
CONVERSATIONS.'

CHERELLE, SERIES ONE

Focus on function

When we first walk into a family's home on the show, all too often we're confused over what a particular room is meant to be. We've seen spaces that are part-living room, part-dining room, part-home office, part-kids' playroom and part-storage for a six-month supply of loo roll all at the same time. Due to space restrictions, the rooms in our homes frequently need to perform multiple functions, which is perfectly achievable through clever zoning, but what we want to avoid are junk-filled rooms with no clear purpose. Focusing on the primary functions of each space brings clarity to your home, so that every room makes sense.

 ## ZONE YOUR HOME

Even when a room has to be multipurpose because of limited space, creating a designated zone for relaxing, eating or playing will keep each area distinct from one another. Think of each zone as a room within a room. You can create separation between zones by using a partition, room divider or other piece of furniture, such as a unit or bookshelves, or you can use colour to subtly mark the shift between one zone and the next. When you zone your home, everyone will better understand the function of that space and know what lives where, making it less likely to return into disorganised chaos.

'OPEN—PLAN LIVING CAN BE WONDERFUL, HOWEVER, IF IT'S NOT CLEARLY ZONED AND THERE'S NO SPACE TO PUT THINGS AWAY, THEN IT CAN BECOME CLUTTERED AND MESSY.'

STACEY

'I MOVE AROUND MY FURNITURE ALL THE TIME BECAUSE SOMETIMES YOU HAVE TO LIVE WITH IT FOR A BIT TO REALISE. "OH, MY GOSH, THIS IS NOT WORKING. I CAN'T EVEN GET TO THAT CUPBOARD." SOMETIMES WE LIVE WITH A LAYOUT THINKING THAT'S THE ONLY OPTION.'

STACEY

ORGANISE THINGS TO MAKE SENSE

At this point, when the room is clear, take a moment to review the layout of the room and the position of the furniture. Forget about where you've always placed the sofa or the bed and consider whether there's another layout that would make the room work better. A space should always flow and cupboards should always be easy to get into!

 ## EXPLOIT ALL STORAGE OPTIONS

Survey the space to identify any spots where some extra hidden storage might be introduced. Under a coffee table, inside a box seat, under a kitchen unit, behind a bath panel, under the stairs and even inside the stairs are just some of the spots where Rob has created clever hidden storage. For more of Rob's genius extra storage ideas used in the show, see page 244.

THE BUFTON FAMILY, SERIES FOUR

* 197 teddies and dolls

* 121 odd socks

* 373 pieces of unopened mail

* 1,239 books

Introduce systems

A household with systems in place runs far more smoothly than one without. To start with, by clearing the clutter you already have less of everything to tidy. And with each item having its own place, you'll find everyone can put their stuff away as they go so the chores get spread throughout the day. As everything is tidied away in its place and all surfaces are clear, it's then possible to whizz round and do a speedy clean-up.

 GIVE EVERY ITEM A DESIGNATED PLACE

'A place for everything and everything in its place.' This is a popular saying, but it rings true. When you have a specific place designated to each and every item, they're more likely to be returned there, not just by you but by every other household member. And the beauty is that the next time you need something, you'll know exactly where it is.

THE SEABROOK FAMILY, SERIES THREE

* 1,066 kids' toys

* 71 pairs of leggings

* 88 towels

* 32 dog bowls

HERO PRODUCT: LABELLING MACHINE

Dilly's labelling machine is the fifth member of the *Sort Your Life Out* team. It's definitely the most-used piece of equipment that helps us organise each home. You might think it's a bit over the top labelling so many things around the home, but if you live in a busy household then it really helps everyone to understand the system. We label every piece of storage, whether it's for breakfast cereal or plastic action figures, so there are no excuses!

'PEOPLE THOUGHT THAT WE WOULD NEVER BE ABLE TO MAINTAIN IT, BUT THE SYSTEMS THE TEAM PUT IN PLACE HAVE MADE IT EASY AND, FOR US, A GAME—CHANGER.'

TASH, *SORT YOUR LIFE OUT* SPECIAL

DISPLAY WHAT YOU CHERISH

Now that you've freed up lots of lovely space by decluttering and everything is organised in a smooth-running system, don't forget to enjoy that space by creating displays of items that you cherish the most. Gallery walls, box frames and floating shelves are all great options, depending on what you want to showcase.

 SYSTEMISE > THE MASTER BEDROOM

Quite often on the show, when we reveal the fully reorganised bedroom to the homeowners, they exclaim, 'Oh, it's like a boutique hotel.' But why do we love fancy hotel rooms so much? It's probably because they are fuss-free and uncluttered, containing only the essentials that we really need. Your bedroom should be a soothing space where you can rest and recharge, so make it a sanctuary away from the stresses of daily life and free from extraneous clutter that doesn't belong there.

ORGANISATION

Think about the placement of furniture in the room and what makes the most sense. With the bed, wardrobe and chest of drawers, some sizeable pieces of furniture are housed in this room. If you don't have built-in wardrobes that limit your options, try a few different arrangements until you find the most practical one. If you can, keep a good amount of circulation space around the bed and always make sure that you can access every cupboard and drawer.

STORAGE

Look at your existing storage and make improvements where you can. What if you adjusted the height of the shelves in your wardrobe? Would that give you better storage options? What if you added an extra hanging rail at a different height? Would that mean you could hang two rows of clothes, one above the other? If you're in the market for a new bed, consider an ottoman bed that can store beneath the mattress lots of items that you don't use every day. And it's a smart idea to have a bedside table with a drawer for keeping those things that you prefer to have close to hand but don't necessarily want on display – medication, sleep mask, sleep spray, etc – so that you can keep the top clear.

WORKING THAT STORAGE

To use every scrap of storage in the most efficient way possible, you're going to need some kit. Without the right hangers, a wardrobe is just a poorly used cupboard. Without dividers, drawers can quickly become a knotted jumble of socks and tights. Get the right supplies in before attempting to store your clothes:

- ❏ EXTRA HANGING RAILS (IF NECESSARY)
- ❏ SLIM CLOTHES HANGERS
- ❏ SLIM CLIP HANGERS OR MULTI–TIERED HANGERS

☐ DRAWER DIVIDERS

☐ DRAWER ORGANISERS

☐ BASKETS OR BOXES

If you have a dressing table where you get ready, you may also need some organisers or containers for make-up and other beauty products that are stored in the bedroom rather than the bathroom.

TIP ✳
MAKE YOUR OWN MULTI–TIERED HANGERS

Instead of spending money on fancy multi-tiered hangers, use ring pulls from drinks cans instead. Separate the ring pull from the drink can, slide one end of the ring pull over one hanger and then slot the hook of a second hanger into the other hole of the ring pull, so that you can double hang garments in your wardrobe and maximise space.

STORING CLOTHES

Whether you choose to hang, fold or roll your clothes to store them will depend on the storage space you have available, but there are some general rules over what to hang and what to fold. It's preferable to hang bulky clothes that won't fold easily, like heavy overcoats and padded jackets, as well as fabrics that are prone to crease. On the flip side, it's not advisable to hang knitwear as the loose structure of the knitted fabric means it can easily be stretched out of shape. However you store your clothes, the most important thing is that everything can be seen at a glance as the only clothes that ever get worn are the ones that you can see. **The golden rule is:** make sure all your clothes are visible so you don't forget what you own.

HANGING CLOTHES

When hanging clothes, group similar types of garments together and arrange them from heavier outerwear down to lighter garments worn closer to the body:

- ❏ OVERCOATS AND RAINCOATS

- ❏ JACKETS AND BLAZERS

- ❏ LONGER DRESSES

- ❏ SHORTER DRESSES

- ❏ SHIRTS, T-SHIRTS AND VESTS

- ❏ JEANS, TROUSERS AND SHORTS (ON CLIP HANGERS OR MULTI-TIERED HANGERS)

- ❏ SKIRTS (ON CLIP HANGERS)

TIP ✳
ORGANISE BY TYPE NOT COLOUR

Always organise your clothes by type and not by colour. A block of black garments followed by a block of red clothes might look good from a distance, but it's not the most helpful system. It's more time-efficient to organise by garment type, so each day you can grab something for your top half and something else for your bottom half, which might not always be the same colour.

On one side, the full-length clothes will hang down almost to the wardrobe floor. But on the other side, where the clothes are shorter, you may be able to fit a second hanging rail mid-way down. If you don't have a space to hang all your full-length garments, then you can use two hangers instead of one to reduce the space needed, but they need to be the type of hanger that has a bar across the bottom. With the top of the garment already on a hanger, hold the clothing up and slide a second hanger over the garment from the bottom up. Stop at knee level and then bring the lower hanger up to meet the other one so the garment is folded upwards.

FOLDING CLOTHES

There are some types of garments that you may prefer to fold and store in a drawer rather than hang, like jeans and t-shirts, and then there are certain small items, like underwear and socks, that you're never going to hang. Drawers can sometimes be quite deep and with a pile of t-shirts inside, stacked one on top of the other, you just can't see every item that's in there as most of the clothes are obscured by the garment sat on top. This is where 'file folding' is your storage saviour. File folding is a method of folding clothes so that every garment stands upright instead of lying flat. Folding clothes this way has three benefits. Firstly, it's incredibly neat with each garment folded into a tight parcel. Secondly, it's brilliantly space-efficient and uses the maximum height of a drawer. And thirdly, you can see every article of clothing in a neat run, like folders in a filing cabinet.

TIP ✳

FAVOURITES AT THE FRONT

Arrange the clothes in your drawers so that the items you wear most frequently are at the front. This way you can reach them quickly without disturbing everything else in the drawer and then they can easily be slotted back in place once laundered.

30-SECOND FOLD: T-SHIRTS, SWEATSHIRTS AND SWEATERS

1. Lay your t-shirt out flat with the back facing upwards and smooth out any creases with your hands.

2. Fold the right edge of the t-shirt including the right sleeve in towards the centre.

3. Fold the left edge of the t-shirt including the left sleeve in towards the centre.

4. Fold the t-shirt in half lengthways so the bottom hem now sits just below the neckband.

5. Fold the t-shirt in half lengthways again so that all the edges are aligned in a neat parcel.

6. Stack the folded t-shirt upright in your drawer or drawer organiser, along with your other t-shirts, so that you can easily see each one.

This folding method for t-shirts can also be used for sweatshirts and knitwear. For longer sleeves, when you fold the sides in towards the centre, fold the sleeve back on itself at the top and then angle it so that it runs vertically down the sweatshirt or jumper towards the hem. For bulky hoodies, fold in the arms as for a sweater and fold the body up one or two times to make it square. Next, tuck the folded body inside the hood and then pull the drawstrings tightly to make a neat parcel. If you're feeling fancy, you can even tie them in a bow.

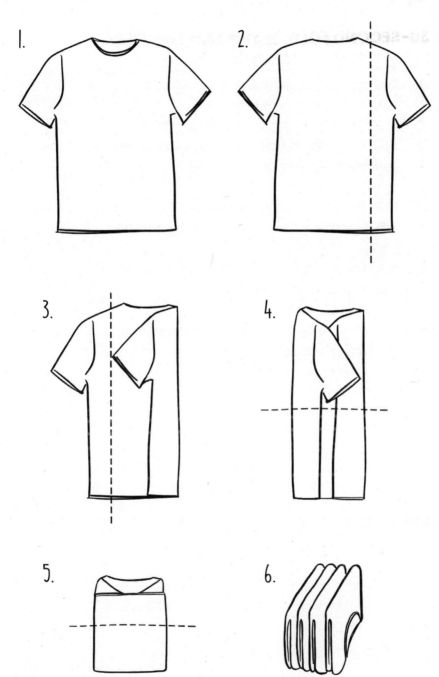

1.

2.

3.

4.

5.

6.

30-SECOND FOLD: JEANS AND TROUSERS

1. Lay your jeans out flat and smooth out any creases in the fabric with your hands.

2. Fold the jeans in half widthways so the two legs are now together with all edges aligned.

3. Fold the jeans in half lengthways so the bottom hems of the legs now sit just beneath the waistband.

4. Fold the jeans in half lengthways again so that all edges are aligned in a neat parcel.

5. Stack the folded jeans in your drawer upright so that you can easily see each pair.

1.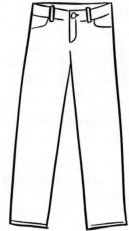

2.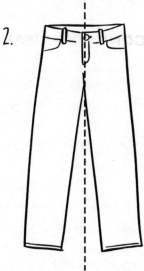

3.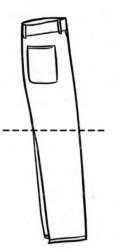

4.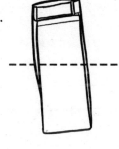

5.

6.

⦀ 30-SECOND FOLD: PANTS

1. Lay your pants out flat with the front facing upwards.

2. Fold the waistband and a little of the main fabric under to sit at the back.

3. Fold the right side in towards the centre. Repeat with the left side.

4. Fold the bottom third up towards the centre, then fold the next third upwards too.

5. Pull the outer edge of the visible waistband from the back over to the front to make a neat parcel.

6. Stack the folded pants in your drawer or drawer organiser upright so that you can easily see each pair.

Once your pants are neatly folded, group them by type so that your everyday cotton pants are together, then the fancy lacy ones or sports ones are together. If the pants have a matching vest, top or bra, keep those sets together.

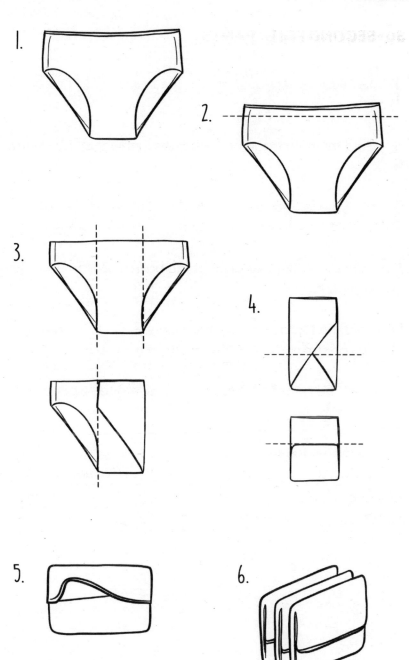

1.

2.

3.

4.

5.

6.

||| 30-SECOND FOLD: BOXERS

1. Lay your boxers out flat with the back facing upwards.

2. Fold the right edge of the boxers in towards the centre.

3. Fold the left edge of the boxers in towards the centre.

4. Fold the bottom quarter of the boxers upwards towards the centre.

5. Fold the top quarter of the boxers down towards the centre.

6. Tuck the bottom hems of the legs into the waistband in the centre.

7. Stack the folded boxers in your drawer or drawer organiser upright so that you can easily see each pair.

1.

2.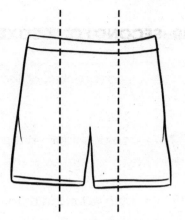

3.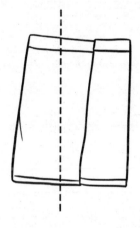

4.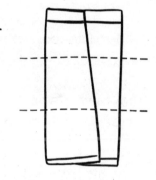

5.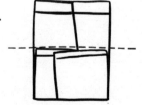

6.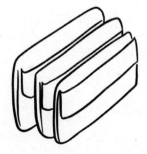

30-SECOND FOLD: SOCKS

1. Lay your socks out flat with the soles facing upwards.

2. Place one sock on top of the other so that the toes of one sock are over the cuff of the other.

3. Fold the bottom third of the socks upwards towards the centre.

4. Fold the next third of the socks upwards again.

5. Pull the outer edge of the visible cuff over itself and the folded socks to make a neat parcel.

6. Stack the folded socks in your drawer or drawer organiser upright so that you can easily see each pair.

This folding method means that the wrong side of the sock is visible, holding the parcel together. If you prefer to clearly see the colour and design of the socks, start with the pair turned inside out. Once your socks are neatly folded, group them by type so that your everyday cotton socks are together, then the sports socks are together, and so on.

1.

2.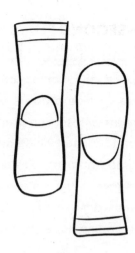

3.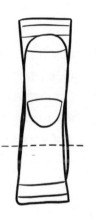

4.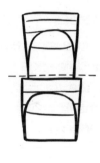

5.

6.

HERO PRODUCT: DRAWER ORGANISERS

Once your clothes are neatly folded, stacking them in organisers inside drawers keeps everything in order. You can buy them with section dividers, so they keep everything from socks and bras to t-shirts and jeans neatly in place and it's easy to grab whatever you want to wear. But you don't need to buy one of these when an empty shoe box will do the job just as well. If you want to make it all look a little prettier, cover the shoe box in wrapping paper or even some scented drawer liner paper.

STORING SHOES

Stack shoes neatly in boxes on the base of your wardrobe or use a free-standing shoe rack. So that you can quickly find the pair you need, see-through boxes are a huge plus, otherwise, stick a photo on the front of the box. For a DIY shoe rack, install a couple of extendable tension rods across the bottom of your wardrobe and balance the shoes across the two rods.

STORING ACCESSORIES

Depending on your dress sense, you may wear lots of accessories or you may have none at all. Handbags, hats, scarves and belts all vary wildly in size, so there are a number of storage options from extra hanging rails to storage boxes, but woven baskets are always a good choice. If you have a collection of handbags, consider a display wall of floating shelves so you can enjoy them even when you're not wearing them. To keep their shape, stuff handbags with tissue paper.

TIPS ✳
STORE AWAY YOUR SEASONAL WARDROBE

Quite a few items of clothing will only be worn during a certain time of the year, so pack away any seasonal items until they're needed. See-through vacuum-sealed bags minimise the amount of space that bulky overcoats and chunky knitwear take up and protect vulnerable fabrics from clothes moths. One downside is that you can't see everything that's in the bag until you open it up, so it's a good idea to label the bag with a list of the clothes it contains.

FORGET THE FLOORDROBE

To avoid a puddle of discarded garments on the bedroom floor, have a system for hanging clothes when you undress at night. For an instant option, you could add a simple self-adhesive hook to the bedroom door. Or you can upgrade to a 'valet hanger' or 'valet hook', which either extends from the wardrobe door or hooks over the top of a door, to provide a handy place to hang worn clothes to air. You can also use a valet hanger or hook to put together outfits for the day ahead, allowing them to hang and any creases to drop.

SYSTEMISE › THE KIDS' BEDROOMS

As your child grows, they're likely to spend more and more time in their own bedroom. As well as for sleeping, they will use the space to play, to read and to do homework, so it needs to be a flexible, multipurpose space. And if you're a parent or guardian, you'll know how much toy debris is usually scattered across the floor after a play session, so good storage is essential.

ORGANISATION

How you arrange the furniture in a kid's room is key to maximising the available floor space, which is crucial if you want to encourage your child to play in their room and save the chaos from spreading to other spaces in the home. Don't be afraid to place a child's bed flat against the wall to free up as much floor space as possible. You'd never usually do that for an adults' double bed, but a child's single bed only needs to be accessed from one side. Likewise, laying a playmat or rug on the floor not only makes it more comfortable but it also defines the play space, so hopefully things don't get spread around too much.

ZONING

If you're squeezed for space and more than one child shares a bedroom, you can still make the space work with clever zoning. Give each child their own space by creating defined areas within the room, carving out individual corners.

REAL LIFE INSPO

In the very first home we ever organised, twins Grace and Elijah shared a bedroom. We gave each of them their own side of the room by mounting large panels of MDF behind their beds that we painted in different but complementary colours. We then personalised those panels even further by hanging framed sheets of wrapping paper printed with their initials, but you could just as easily hang a framed poster or football shirt. This is a really cost-effective way of zoning the space, and it can easily be updated as the kids get older.

Alternatively, follow Stacey's upcycling idea for personalising a kid's bedroom with a decorated initial. Take a wooden letter bought from a craft supplier, paint it if you prefer and then decorate it by gluing a selection of the child's model cars or other toys that are duplicates or no longer played with. You need to use strong adhesive and leave it to dry for at least an hour. Hang the decorated initial on the wall or rest it on a shelf over their bed. Using their own toys makes it personal to them and frees up space.

Zoning the space is something that you may want to consider even when a child has a room to themself. Depending on their age, it's useful to have zones for playing, reading and studying, as well as sleeping. This is done partly by the placement of furniture, but colour can also help to define a space. Self-adhesive wallpaper is a fun way of bringing colour and pattern into a room. You don't have to stick with straight panels as the paper can be cut into shapes with a sharp retractable blade. And what's more, it peels away easily when you want to remove or change it.

REAL LIFE INSPO

When we visited the Watling family home in series three, we created a quiet reading space for Aria in the bedroom she shared with her younger sister Nerea. We did this with an inexpensive bed canopy hung from the ceiling in one corner of the room to create a private area. Alongside the reading tent, we positioned a kids' bookcase for all of Aria's favourite books. The books all sit with their front cover face out, meaning your child can pick out what they want to read, which is trickier when they can only see the spines of the books.

STORING TOYS

We deal with storing toys a bit later on in the section on kids' play spaces (see page 195), but a bedroom is the usual place you'll find soft toys. Encourage your child to choose the toys they most love to hug and then gather them together in a 'cuddle basket'. This stops them emptying out their entire toy box looking for that one teddy, and it encourages them to put everything back in the basket so they're to hand for the next cuddle session. Another way of saving space is to fill a bean bag with soft toys, so that it doubles as storage as well as usable seating.

STORING CLOTHES

The same organisational principles apply to kids' clothes as they do to adults' clothes. Group similar items together and fold everything neatly to use the available storage space in the most efficient way possible. In a kid's room, labelling every section of a drawer is a really great idea as it means they know where everything is and it encourages them to dress themselves and put their own clothes away, giving them more independence and boosting their confidence. If your kids are very young and don't yet read, try using picture labels with simple outlines of each type of garment. However, if you have more than one child of similar ages, rather than organising and labelling clothes by name, arrange them by age as it's easier if they share rather than have their own separate sock drawers.

FOLDING CLOTHES

As most kids' garments are miniature versions of adult clothing, you can use the same folding methods starting on page 138. The exception is baby clothes, however, with all-in-one babygrows needing their own folding technique.

30-SECOND FOLD: BABYGROWS

1. Lay the babygrow out flat with the front facing upwards.

2. Fold the right arm inwards so that it sits over the body. Repeat with the left arm.

3. Fold the right leg upwards so that it sits over the body. Repeat with the left leg.

4. Fold the babygrow in half widthways so the two sides of the body are now together with all edges aligned.

5. Fold the bottom third of the babygrow up towards the centre.

6. Fold the next third of the babygrow upwards again.

7. Stack the folded babygrows in your drawer upright so that you can easily see each one.

1.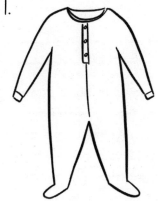

2.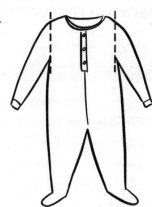

3.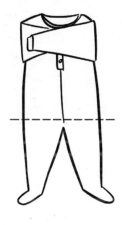

4.

5.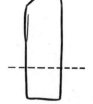

6.

7.

TIP ✳
HANDLING HAND—ME—DOWNS

Any family with more than one child is going to hand down clothes from the older to the younger kids. They grow so fast it feels like most of their clothes are barely worn before they need the next size up. This is where the dot system is your friend. Using a fabric marker pen (make sure it's washable), draw a dot on the label of each garment worn by the youngest child, but don't mark the clothes worn by the eldest child. Then, when the older child grows out of their gear and it's passed down to their younger sibling, mark that garment with a dot. So, without a dot means oldest child, with a dot means youngest child. This system also makes putting laundry away a breeze as they can see instantly which clothes are theirs.

SYSTEMISE > THE BATHROOM

The bathroom is a practical space where we energise for the day ahead of us and then unwind after the day behind us. For both of these things to happen, we need an organised space.

ORGANISATION

As all the fixtures are plumbed in, there's less flexibility in the bathroom when it comes to reorganisation. Instead, we need to look at ways to make the space work better and introduce some clever storage, where needed.

STORAGE

If you already have cupboards in the bathroom, check that the shelves are all at the best heights for whatever you're storing and adjust them, if necessary. Next, check for any spaces where you can carve out extra storage. You may want to consider adding some shelving or free-standing units, if you have space.

REAL LIFE INSPO

For Steph and her three girls in series one, Rob cleverly added more built-in storage hidden behind the bath panel so they each had their own space behind push-close doors.

WORKING STORAGE

While you might not have the space to add built-in cupboards to your bathroom, it's a great room for using wicker hampers, wire baskets or wire wastepaper bins for storing everything from face cloths to loo rolls. So, get kitted out with those bits and bobs that will help you use your available space in the most effective way possible:

- ❑ WICKER HAMPERS

- ❑ WIRE BASKETS OR WIRE WASTEPAPER BINS

- ❑ SHOWER CADDY

- ❑ PLASTIC CONTAINERS OR ORGANISERS

- ❑ GLASS DISPLAY JARS OR PUMP—ACTION DISPENSERS

- ❑ LOCKBOX FOR MEDICINES

STORING BATHROOM PRODUCTS

How you organise the products in your bathroom is up to you. Go with whichever system makes the most sense for you and your family, which might differ according to whether you each have your own products or share the same ones.

If you all share, then it makes sense to organise all the products into groups according to usage:

- ❏ HAIR CARE PRODUCTS
- ❏ SKIN CARE PRODUCTS
- ❏ BODY WASH AND SHOWER GEL
- ❏ SHAVING PRODUCTS
- ❏ DENTAL PRODUCTS
- ❏ MEDICINES

However, if you each have your own self-care regime, then you might prefer to organise them according to your daily routine:

- ❏ MORNING ROUTINE PRODUCTS
- ❏ EVENING ROUTINE PRODUCTS
- ❏ OCCASIONAL USE PRODUCTS

TIP ✳
STORE MEDICINES SAFELY

It's vitally important that all medicines are stored safely and out of harm's way. Even if you don't have children living in your home, you may have pets and occasional visitors that could access any medicines left in reach. So, store all medicines and first-aid items together on a high shelf or at the top of a tall cupboard where children cannot grab them. Or, even better, stow medicines away in a lockbox that is kept up high.

FOLDING TOWELS

For fresh towels not in use, you may want to store them in the bathroom so they're to hand when needed. Towels can be neatly folded and stacked on a shelf, with the largest bath sheets on the bottom of the stack, or they can be rolled and stored in a basket.

|||| 30-SECOND FOLD: TOWELS

1. Fold the towel in half lengthways so that all edges are aligned.

2. Fold the top third of the towel down towards the centre.

3. Fold the bottom third of the towel up towards the centre.

4. Fold the left side of the towel in towards the centre.

5. Fold the right side of the towel in to meet the open edge of the left side and neatly tuck it all the way in.

6. Stack the folded towels on a shelf. When in use, you can tuck your toiletries into the flap on the front of the folded towel parcel to transport them conveniently.

1.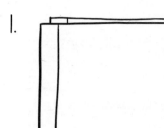

2.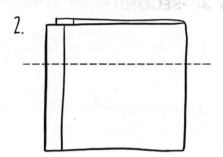

3.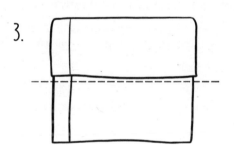

4.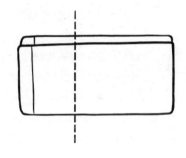

5.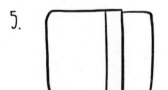

6.

⫼ 30-SECOND ROLL: TOWELS

1. Fold the towel in half lengthways so that all edges are aligned.

2. Fold the top left corner down towards the centre of the towel.

3. Fold the bottom right corner up to meet the sloping edge at the top left of the towel.

4. Take the bottom left corner of the towel under and along so that it sits beneath the top right corner, but slightly offset. You don't want the edges to be perfectly aligned.

5. Roll the towel into a tight log, working from the straight edge towards the pointed corner.

6. When the towel is completely rolled, the pointed corner should be just over a v-shaped fold.

7. Tuck the pointed corner firmly into the v-shaped fold to secure.

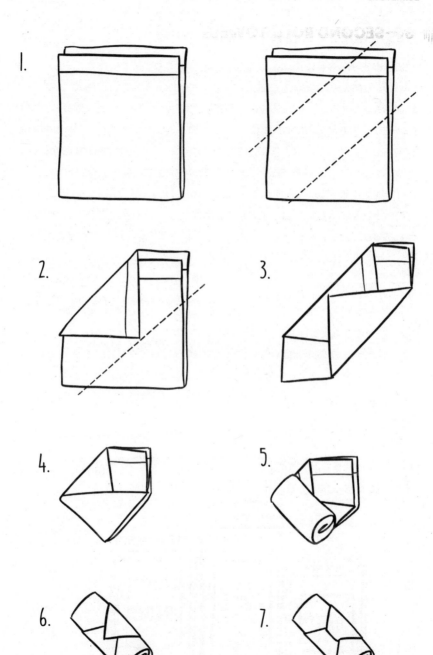

SYSTEMISE > THE KITCHEN

The kitchen is the hub of the home. It's a place not just where meals are prepared, but also where packed lunches are handed over with a kiss on the head, where consoling cups of tea are drunk, and where a kitchen disco is enjoyed in between stirring the spag bol. It's the command centre for family life, and as such It needs to be organised and the space needs to flow. Of all the rooms in the home, organising the kitchen is most likely the biggest task, so don't try to rush it and set aside plenty of time. You may even need to do it over a few days.

ORGANISATION

The ideal kitchen is a well-organised space with a layout that flows, with adequate storage and that's easy to keep clean. Consider the set-up of your kitchen and how easy it is to move around while you're cooking. Have you heard of the kitchen work triangle? It's a well-known principle in kitchen design that when the hob, fridge and sink are arranged in a triangle then that gives you the most efficient workflow. If moving your fridge would improve the layout, do it.

TIP ✳
ADD COLOUR TO YOUR WHITE GOODS

White goods don't need to be white. If you have to house a fridge or freezer in a certain space, you can always cover the door in a coloured vinyl wrap to make it blend in better with the decor.

ZONING

It can pay to zone the space in your kitchen by function. Think about allocating an area for food preparation, another for cooking and then another for cleaning products, if you don't have a utility room. Keep utensils like your vegetable peeler near to the sink, where you prepare vegetables. Pots, pans and cooking utensils are best kept close to the hob and oven. And if you can store crockery, cutlery and glassware near to the dishwasher, unloading everything will be a breeze. Keep your most used plates, bowls and cups within easy reach so that you're not reaching up to high shelves to bring down heavy crockery.

STORAGE

As the kitchen has to house a lot of stuff, from pots and pans to teaspoons, finding nifty ways of fitting more into the space is key. Consider every available area from floor to ceiling. Use every spare inch, including those up high as well as at floor level.

REAL LIFE INSPO

In Bijal and Darshan's home in series one, Rob fitted some extra pull-out drawers in the otherwise unused space behind the base plinths of the kitchen units. These were standard flatpack drawers fitted with castors so they could be pulled out smoothly. Overflow baking equipment that was only occasionally used is now stored there, freeing up regular cupboard space for more frequently used items.

If you're working with what you already have in terms of kitchen cupboards, always adjust the height of the shelves to suit what you're storing there. For example, in the cupboard next to the hob, it's a smart idea to make sure you can house tall bottles of oil that you can grab easily when cooking.

'WHENEVER I GO INTO A HOUSE, I ALWAYS ADJUST THE SHELVES. PEOPLE MOVE INTO THEIR KITCHEN AND JUST PUT THINGS AWAY FORGETTING THAT THE SHELVES MOVE. IF THAT SHELF MOVED UP ONE MORE NOTCH, YOU COULD FIT OILS AND VINEGARS IN HERE NEXT TO THE HOB.'

DILLY

WORKING THE STORAGE

There are a number of must-have accessories that really make the difference in a kitchen as they maximise the available storage space and make it easier to access what you need. Consider adding the following to your shopping list when preparing to systemise your kitchen:

- ❏ MULTI–TIER PLATE RACKS

- ❏ OVER–THE–DOOR PAN LID RACKS OR STICK–ON PAN LID HOLDERS

- ❏ STEPPED SHELF ORGANISERS

- ❏ LAZY SUSAN OR TURNTABLE

- ❏ ADJUSTABLE DRAWER DIVIDERS

- ❏ DRAWER ORGANISERS

- ❏ UNDER–CABINET KITCHEN ROLL HOLDER

- ❏ STORAGE BASKETS OR BOXES

- ❏ SEE–THROUGH FOOD STORAGE CONTAINERS WITH AIRTIGHT LIDS

- ❏ SET OF PRE–PRINTED PANTRY LABELS OR LABELLING MACHINE

TIPS ✳

HEAVIEST AT THE BOTTOM

In almost all kitchens, you'll find a run of base units, including some with deep drawers, and then above the countertop there will most likely be some wall-mounted cabinets and perhaps open shelving. It makes the most sense to store the heaviest items, like your cast-iron casserole dish, in the lower units so that you aren't lifting something that weighs a lot down from up high. The opposite applies to lighter, more fragile items, like drinking glasses. These are best stored above the countertop so there is less risk of something falling onto and breaking them. **The golden rule is:** store the heaviest items in the lower units and any lighter items up high.

HANG PANS AND LIDS

One exception to this golden rule is if you install a hanging system for pans and utensils. This could be a single rail mounted on the wall above a hob with butcher's hooks for hanging pans by their handles or an industrial-looking pot rack that can be suspended over a kitchen island. Another space-saving tip is to install either an over-the-door pan lid rack or stick-on pan lid holders to the inside of the unit door. The lids slot into the spaces, keeping them organised and in easy reach.

GLASS ORDER

When organising delicate glassware in wall cabinets or on shelves, place your least-used glasses on the highest shelf and most-used glasses on the lowest shelf at eye level. You don't want to have to go on tiptoes to reach for a glass every time you need a drink.

CUPBOARD ACCESSIBILITY

Make every cupboard as accessible as possible. Use multi-tier plate racks in the base units to break up heavy stacks of plates and bowls, so they're easy to grab. Likewise, use stepped shelf organisers in wall cabinets so that the items at the back are raised up and fully visible – like they're sat in the posh seats at the theatre!

DRAWER ORGANISERS

Adjustable drawer dividers are great for sectioning off wide kitchen drawers, so items stay in their designated sections rather than migrating into a mixed-up mess. Likewise, drawer organisers with different-sized compartments can be used for more than just cutlery. You can even buy a specially designed junk drawer organiser with compartments for scissors, sticky tape and batteries. And on the subject of junk drawers, be strict and only allow one drawer for those odd items that don't have a place elsewhere.

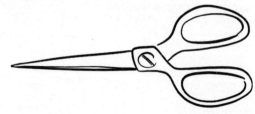

MAKE A KIDS' DRAWER

Make one of the lower-height drawers in the kitchen the kids' drawer for storing sippy cups and other child-friendly bits and pieces. If they can help themselves to a cup or whatever else they need, it gets them into the habit of helping around the home and is an empowering confidence-boost for them.

A LAZY SUSAN

Another game-changing accessory is the lazy Susan – a spinning turntable – which whizzes around so that you don't have to move lots of items to find the one thing you need.

In the kitchen, a lazy Susan can transform your cupboards and fridge. By placing all those jars, packets or tins (that usually get forgotten about because they're stuck at the back of the shelf) on a rotating turntable, you can instantly see and access what you need with a spin of the wheel. No more clearing the entire shelf to reach that one thing. And no more wasted food that goes out of date because you forget it's there.

'THERE IS NO NEED FOR MORE THAN ONE JUNK DRAWER. I UNDERSTAND THAT LIFE IS BUSY, TIMES ARE TOUGH AND YOU'VE GOT TO SWEEP IT ALL INTO ONE PLACE AT SOME POINT, BUT IT SHOULDN'T TAKE OVER YOUR WHOLE KITCHEN.'

STACEY

REAL LIFE INSPO

The team needed to find a way of utilising the space in Aimee and Stuart's newly emptied garage, somewhere to store the overspilling food and drink that was previously cluttering up the under-stairs cupboard where they couldn't see what they had, which led to overbuying. The ideal solution was a storage unit that rotates – like a super-sized lazy Susan. Inside the unit, a series of segmented compartments were rested on a lazy Susan mechanism so that the whole thing spun inside the cupboard.

STORING APPLIANCES

During the sort stage, you decided to keep only those small appliances that you can't live without. In order to keep your countertops clear, have permanently out just those appliances that you use on a daily – or at the very least weekly – basis. That might be your kettle, coffee machine and toaster, and perhaps an air fryer or microwave if you regularly use one as an alternative to a conventional oven. For any other appliance you use infrequently, you'll need to find some cupboard space to store it away when not in use.

STORING FOOD

A cluttered, disorganised fridge, freezer and kitchen cupboards can lead to food waste as you're never sure how much you have in stock and so end up buying blind. Implement the following systems to minimise wasting food and money:

✳ **Organise your fridge using dishwasher-safe drawer dividers and labelled storage containers** – keep all the same food types together, such as all your cheese in one container. This is not only for maximum efficiency but also for food safety as it prevents cross-contamination between raw and cooked foods.

✳ **Label every freezer section or drawer** – this makes it a lot easier for everyone to put things back properly.

✳ **Label every freezer container** – if you batch cook or freeze leftovers, add the contents of the container and date it was stored. You always think you'll remember what's in that tub or ziplock bag, but once it's in the freezer and frosted up a spag bol and a chilli con carne look identical.

✳ **Keep a freezer inventory** – if you note down everything that's in your freezer, you'll know exactly what you've got and when it needs to be used up. This way, you're more likely to use up all your freezer foods before they go out of date.

✳ **Arrange all perishable food items in date order** – think like a supermarket and make sure that those items with the closest use-by dates are placed at the front of the fridge, freezer or cupboard so they get used up first.

✳ **Make a 'TO EAT NEXT' container** – add in all the store cupboard foods that are going to expire within the next month and label it 'TO EAT NEXT' so that it catches your eye whenever you're planning a meal. You can do the same with fresh foods in the fridge (but avoiding cross-contamination) for those items that are best eaten within the next week.

✳ **Decant store cupboard foods into see-through containers with airtight containers** – because they're see-through, you can tell when they're getting near to empty and it's time to top up. An added bonus of using a storage container with an airtight lid is that the food stays fresher for longer.

✳ **If you store dried goods on open shelving, decant them into decorative jars** – a row of labelled jars always looks better than a mismatched assortment of packaging. Even a few old pickle jars can look just as smart as Kilner jars.

✳ **Store carrier bags in an old tissue box** – we all end up with a load of plastic carrier bags, no matter how hard we try to remember our bag for life. An empty tissue box makes a handy dispenser, and if they don't all fit in the box, then the extras get recycled.

✳ **Make a chalkboard door** – rather than spoil the outside of the cabinets or fridge with a series of Post-it notes, paint the inside of one of the wall-mounted cupboards with chalkboard paint. This gives you a place to write shopping lists or other important notes while keeping the visible door fronts clean and clear.

HERO PRODUCT: SEE—THROUGH FOOD STORAGE CONTAINERS WITH AIRTIGHT LIDS

Whether you use purpose-made storage tubs with pop-button lids or recycle washed-out glass pickle jars with screw-on lids, transferring your cereal, pasta, rice and other grains and pulses from their packets into see-through containers really does make a difference. At a glance, you'll be able to see when you're about to run out of an ingredient and need to restock, rather than grabbing more packets when at the supermarket and ending up with far too much of one thing. This immediately cuts down overbuying. Ask the kids to remind you when their favourite cereal is running out or, even better, get them to add it to the shopping list themselves. Don't forget to label each jar, either with a stick-on label or a marker pen specially for writing on glass or plastic. One handy tip is to write on the back of the container the cooking times for each pasta, rice, etc.

FOLDING TECHNIQUES

The kitchen isn't a place where too many different textiles that need folding are kept, but while you might only have one or two kitchen aprons, you probably have a few more tea towels. There's no ideal number of tea towels – it depends on how many you use every week and how frequently you wash them. Folding them neatly means they don't take up too much drawer space, which should be close to the cooking and clean-up zones so they're on hand whenever you need to grab a fresh one.

⦀ 30-SECOND FOLD: TEA TOWELS

1. Lay the tea towel out flat and smooth out any creases with your hands.

2. Fold the right third of the tea towel in towards the centre.

3. Fold the left third of the tea towel in towards the centre.

4. Fold the tea towel in half lengthways so the edges are aligned.

5. Fold the bottom third of the tea towel up towards the centre.

6. Fold the top third of the tea towel down towards the centre to make a neat parcel.

7. Stack the folded tea towels in your drawer upright so that you can see each one.

1.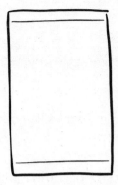

2.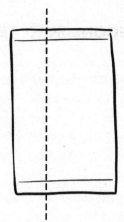

3.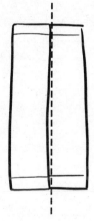

4.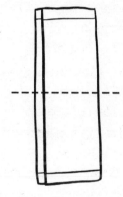

5.

6.

7.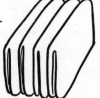

⫼ 30-SECOND FOLD: APRONS

1. Lay the apron out flat with the front facing downwards.

2. Fold the apron in half widthways so the sides are together and edges are aligned.

3. Fold the apron in half widthways again and arrange the waist ties inwards so they sit over the skirt of the apron.

4. Fold the top third of the apron (the bib) down towards the centre and arrange the neck strap so it sits over the skirt of the apron.

5. Fold the next third of the apron down again towards the bottom of the apron, but slightly offset. You don't want the edges to be perfectly aligned.

6. Fold the apron in half again to make a neat parcel.

7. Stack the folded aprons in your drawer upright so that you can see each one.

You might always wear an apron when cooking, but then again you might just embrace the mess and not bother! Or it could be that your kids have their own mini aprons to protect their clothing when helping out with the baking or crafting. Either way, if you don't have a space to hang them up, aprons can be easily folded into a neat parcel to tuck away in the drawer with the tea towels.

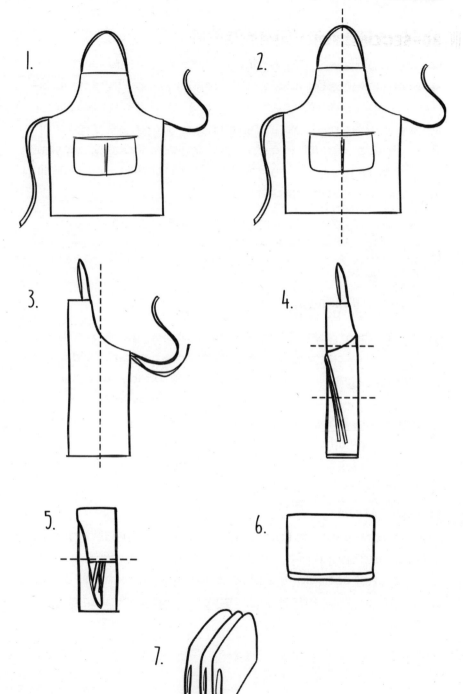

1.

2.

3.

4.

5.

6.

7.

SYSTEMISE > THE UTILITY ROOM

For those of us who live in modest homes, a utility room may seem an impossible luxury. If you're lucky enough to have one, make proper use of it. A utility room is not just a space for storing kitchen overspill, it should have its own clear function. The purpose of a utility room is primarily for laundry, but you may choose to store other things in here too, like your recycling bins and any pet-related items.

BIN BULK BUYING

A utility room often becomes a space for storing bulk buys. Yes, it can be much cheaper to buy multipacks, but you should only bulk buy what you have the space to comfortably store. Check that what you're bulk buying doesn't have an expiry date and how long before it goes off. Remember, things like cleaning wipes do dry out over time.

ORGANISATION

How you organise the space in your utility room will depend on the size and shape of the room and what you make its primary purpose, but consider the practical ways in which you can make the space perfectly functional. Make a list of what you need to store in here:

- ❏ WASHING MACHINE
- ❏ DRYING RACK AND/OR TUMBLE DRYER
- ❏ IRONING BOARD AND IRON
- ❏ LAUNDRY PRODUCTS
- ❏ VACUUM CLEANER AND/OR FLOOR CLEANER
- ❏ CLEANING PRODUCTS
- ❏ HOUSEHOLD ITEMS, SUCH AS LIGHTBULBS AND BATTERIES
- ❏ PET SUPPLIES
- ❏ RECYCLING BOXES OR BINS

As with the kitchen, look at using the full height of the room with floor-to-ceiling cupboards. If it's safe to do so, stack your tumble dryer on top of your washing machine to free up space. Otherwise, fit some suitable shelving around and above the appliances for laundry baskets and washing powder, liquid or pods. If there's not enough room for a tumble dryer, or you prefer not to use one, then look to fit a retractable clothesline or drying rack that extends from the wall, or a retro-style, laundry maid pulley clothes airer that hangs from the ceiling. Another space-saving laundry idea is to fit a drop-down ironing board that stows neatly away or use a half-size ironing board.

STORING LAUNDRY AND LAUNDRY PRODUCTS

Installing storage baskets, one for each family member with their name on, in the laundry area is a game-changer. Once the clothes are dry, they can go in the appropriate basket and it's down to that person to take the basket to their room, then fold and put away their own clothes. This shares the workload and saves piles of clothes being left on the steps to be taken upstairs, which everyone simply steps over as they miraculously cannot see them. Similarly, if you create three large washing bags for dirty clothes – one for darks, one for whites and one for colours – the rest of the family can then be responsible for adding their worn clothes to the correct bag ready for washing.

When it comes to storing laundry products, the most important thing is to store them safely. Keep boxes of laundry detergent, including powder, liquid and especially pods, fabric softener and stain removers out of reach of children and pets.

STORING CLEANING PRODUCTS

The most convenient way to store cleaning products is in a caddy, which you can carry to whatever room you're tackling and then sits neatly in a cupboard when not in use. If you've streamlined your cleaning products to the essentials listed on page 55, they should all fit in a single caddy, but you might prefer to have a few extra dirt-busting weapons in your cleaning arsenal. You could have one caddy for the bathroom and kitchen and then another caddy for the living room and bedrooms, as you'll likely use some different products for the varying surfaces. Another option is to have three separate caddies for those products that you use daily, weekly and monthly. The good thing about organising cleaning products by how often you use them is that the caddy itself acts as a reminder of what needs cleaning at any particular time. Whichever system you use, label each caddy clearly with how and where it's meant to be used.

STORING BED LINENS

With ongoing changes in how we heat our homes, the airing cupboard is increasingly a thing of the past. Ditto the linen cupboard. If the utility room is your best option, you might choose to store your bed linens here. As with towels, you really don't need that many sets of bedlinens. You can make do with three sets per bed – one on the bed, one in the laundry and one spare. For ease, keep each part of a set together – fitted sheet, flat top sheet (if you use one), duvet cover and pillowcases – and tuck everything inside one of the pillowcases so that it makes a neat parcel and is easy to grab when you need to remake the bed. If you don't have a suitable cupboard for storing linens, lift the mattress at the foot of the bed and store the pillow parcel of bedlinen under the mattress where it will be kept nice and flat, plus it's ready to grab whenever the bed needs changing.

||| 30-SECOND FOLD: DUVET SETS

1. Lay the duvet cover out flat and smooth out any creases with your hands.

2. Fold the duvet cover in half widthways so the sides are together and edges aligned.

3. Fold the bottom half of the duvet cover up to sit over the top half.

4. Turn the folded parcel 90 degrees clockwise.

5. Fold the bottom third of the duvet cover up towards the centre. Repeat with the top third, but slightly offset. You don't want the edges to be perfectly aligned.

6. Fold the right side of the duvet cover in towards the centre.

7. Fold the left side of the duvet cover in to meet the open edge of the right side and neatly tuck it all the way in.

8. Slide the folded duvet cover inside one of the matching pillowcases to keep the set together.

1.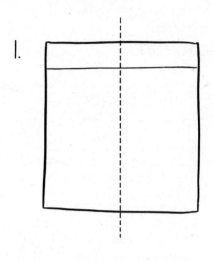

2.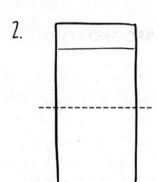

3.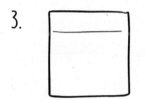

4.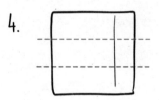

5.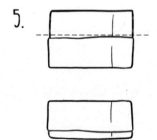

6.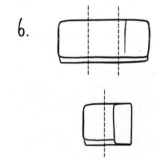

7.

8.

⦀ 30-SECOND FOLD: FITTED BED SHEETS

1. Lay the fitted sheet out flat so that the right side is facing downwards but the elasticated corners are visible on top.

2. Fold the elasticated corners in both bottom corners under and inwards.

3. Fold the bottom half of the sheet upwards and tuck the elasticated corners underneath the elasticated corners at the top.

4. Fold the right third of the sheet in towards the centre.

5. Fold the left third of the sheet in towards the centre.

6. Fold the top third of the sheet with the curved edge in towards the centre.

7. Fold the bottom third of the sheet with the straight edge in towards the centre.

8. Slide the folded fitted sheet inside one of the matching pillowcases to keep the set together.

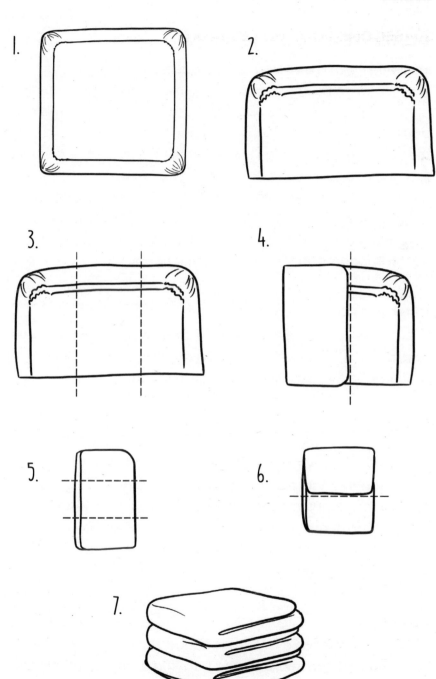

SYSTEMISE > THE LIVING ROOM

The living room is a shared family space and, as such, needs to work for everyone. That might involve making it a child-friendly play area during the day and then transforming it into a relaxing adult space in the evening. It may need to double up as a dining room if there's not enough space in the kitchen or another area for a table to eat around, or you may need to incorporate a desk for homeworking or a spot where you can indulge in your hobbies. While the living room needs to be practical and work hard to provide everything you need, don't forget to make space for the important things that make you happy.

ORGANISATION

Usually, the living room is the largest single space in the home and, as such, is a flexible area with multiple options. Play around with the layout, focusing on what are your primary needs for the space. If you're a family that gathers together on the sofa for movie night, you might want to arrange the furniture so that the sofa is well positioned to see the TV or projector screen. Or if you all love to cosy up in front of the fire for family chats or quiet reading, then armchairs grouped around the fireplace might work best for you all. Work out what the focal point of the room is and then orientate everything towards that. However you place the furniture, make sure that it flows and everyone can move around easily.

ZONING

If your living room is a multi-use space, zoning is your friend. To demarcate the relaxing area from the dining area from the homeworking area, consider the position of the furniture and also the use of floor coverings and wall colour. A freestanding unit can act as a room divider or, failing that, the back of the sofa can make the distinction between zones. Grouping a sofa, armchairs and coffee table so that they sit on a large floor rug immediately ties them all together to make a seating zone. Similarly, the use of colour can subtly distinguish where one zone ends and another begins.

STORAGE

How much furniture you introduce to the living room will again depend on how you use the space. If you entertain regularly, then a sideboard or drinks cabinet might be in order. If you're a family of gamers, then a TV unit that neatly houses a games console helps to keep things tidy. If playing board games is your thing, then a coffee table that doubles as a storage box is the perfect spot to store the Scrabble set.

DISPLAYING PHOTOGRAPHS, ARTWORKS AND COLLECTABLES

There should always be space in your life, and your living room, for those objects that fill you with joy. These might be photographs of loved ones, treasured artworks collected over years or souvenirs picked up on foreign travels. Display whatever is personal to you. Consider some bespoke shelving to properly display your favourite framed photos, collectables or other possessions. Floating shelves are easy to put up, give lots of flexibility and can bear a surprising amount of weight. If your precious objects are fragile and you want to deter people from handling them, position the shelves fairly high up so everything is out of arm's reach.

If you have a lot of photographs, works of art or even decorative plates, grouping them as a gallery wall makes an impactful visual statement. Before you fix anything to the wall, draw the outline of each piece onto a roll of kraft paper and cut the shapes out to make accurate templates. Use some poster putty to temporarily stick these paper templates to the wall to plot the arrangement of your display. To avoid making any unnecessary holes in the wall, only drill the holes for hanging hooks or nails once you're happy with the layout.

TIPS ✳

FORK HANGING TRICK

When hanging pictures, don't scratch around trying to find the picture hook or nail as you might damage the paintwork. Pop a fork onto the hook or nail and then slide the hanging string over the fork handle until it slides down in position.

KID'S ART GALLERY

If you love to put your kid's artwork on display, use an easy-change picture frame and swap the drawing or painting in the frame as they bring a new one home. If any artwork proves to be a particular favourite, it can be made part of a small permanent collection. Similarly, a clipboard stuck to the wall with Command strips can be used to display kids' artworks, which can be quickly and easily unclipped and then a new one put in place.

STORING DVDS AND CDS

If you have chosen to hold on to any DVDs and CDs, to reduce the amount of space that they take up you can buy folders to store the discs in. Simply slide the disc into the specially designed pocket along with the accompanying booklet, then recycle the old plastic case.

 ## SYSTEMISE > THE KIDS' PLAY SPACE

We've already touched on kids' play spaces in the bedroom section, but it's worth repeating here. The better you can confine kids' toys to one area, the more likely you are to save the rest of your home from the debris left after a play session.

ORGANISATION

Create a play zone for the kids, with a playmat on the floor. A foam rug or playmat is wipeable and soft for crawling toddlers. Make sure there is storage for toys right nearby the playmat. If you keep the mat and storage together, then your child is more likely to play right there rather than scatter toys across the room. If your child doesn't play on the sofa and leave their toys everywhere, then when you come to relax, you're more likely to sit on the sofa without finding an action figure up your bum!

REAL LIFE INSPO

If your living room doubles up as the kids' play area during the day, try to make any toys or toy storage blend in with the décor when not in use. Cece's favourite toy kitchen couldn't be wheeled away in the evenings when parents Char and Dan wanted to relax, but it could be turned around to face the wall. So, Rob put a wooden back on it that helped to make it disappear into the room.

STORING TOYS

✳ **Don't keep too many toys** – an excessive number of toys can become overwhelming for a child, so a decluttered space may help them to remain calm and feel more grounded.

✳ **Don't have every toy on show** – similarly, a child can feel overwhelmed by seeing all of their toys at the same time, so store kids' toys in opaque storage rather than see-through containers so that they can concentrate on the one thing they are currently playing with instead of getting distracted. This is especially useful for kids who struggle to focus.

✳ **Group toys by type** – keep all the dinosaurs together, all the action figures together, and so on. If your kids know what the system is and that all the dinosaurs go in this storage box, basket or drawer, they can help put everything back in the place when they're done playing.

* **Use picture labels** – for very young children who are still learning to read, label toy storage with picture labels, so they can understand what goes where without having to read words.

* **Rotate toys** – store a percentage of your kid's toys out of sight and then every month or so swap them over with the ones that have most recently been played with. This helps to keep things fresh and your child will be excited to see those toys that they haven't played with for a while, almost as if they're new.

HERO PRODUCT: CHALKBOARD WALL STICKERS

A removable chalkboard wall sticker provides a place where your kid can draw freely with permission, so it may just save the paintwork on the rest of your walls.

||| SYSTEMISE > THE WORKSPACE/HOME OFFICE

With working from home increasingly becoming the norm, whether full-time or hybrid, it pays to have a quiet space for work or study. For the families we've helped on the show, we've carved out a home office in every size and shape of space, from entire rooms where a business is run to a tiny area on a landing, and even an office-inside-a-cupboard situated in the living room.

ORGANISATION

Depending on the nature of your work, you may not need that big a space for your home office. It could be that a clear surface to place a laptop and a comfortable chair that gives you good support is enough. However, the psychological benefit of having a designated home office space is important because as soon as you sit down at the desk, it signals that you have switched from at-home mode to at-work mode.

REAL LIFE INSPO

At Tash and Lawrence's house, there was never a space for Tash to do her studying, so she ended up working perched on the end of their bed or even sat on the floor. Rob made a home office within a cupboard for Tash, with a pull-out drawer section that acts as a desktop. As well as Tash having a comfortable, custom-made space to study, it also signals to the rest of the family that she is busy and not to be interrupted. And when Tash is done with her studies for the day, the cupboard doors can be closed and every-thing study or work-related is hidden away, allowing Tash to relax.

STORAGE

Even if you don't need a lot to do your paid work or studies, there are still tasks that need to be completed as part of your home admin duties. You'll need some stationery supplies and a system for filing those papers that cannot be recycled. An accordion file with labelled tabs is a good option for filing away those papers that you'll need to refer to in the relatively near future.

HERO PRODUCT: PEGBOARD ORGANISER

A sheet of pegboard makes a cost-effective storage wall in an office or study space. The holes drilled into the pegboard means that you can add custom-made accessories like pen holders, letter holders, display shelves, hooks and clips. For a cost-effective alternative, you can also use bungee cords to hold large items in place on the pegboard. As well as being great for a home office, a pegboard storage wall is equally useful for a hobby desk to organise craft supplies or in a bedroom to keep accessories or make-up all neatly together in one space.

STORING PAPERWORK

It's time to put a system in place for all those bits of paper that you sorted in the previous stage, which you've already categorised into three separate piles:

❑ ACTION

❑ FILE – THIS IS THE PILE FOR ANYTHING THAT DOESN'T NEED IMMEDIATE ACTION, BUT YOU MAY NEED TO REFERENCE IN THE FUTURE.

❑ ARCHIVE – THIS IS THE PILE OF THINGS THAT YOU REALLY CANNOT LET GO OF BECAUSE OF SENTIMENTAL REASONS, SO THEY'LL BE ARCHIVED.

ACTION

Anything that is in the action pile needs to be dealt with asap. The ideal scenario is that each piece of paper in the pile is only ever touched once, so pay it, sign and return it, reply to it or make the callback and then either recycle or file it. If the action you take then requires a follow-up response, move the paper to the bottom of the action pile until further action is needed. As the paperwork in the action pile is 'live', rather than file it away, keep it in an in-tray on your desk.

TIP
IN-TRAY

Any incoming mail and paperwork to be actioned should go in an in-tray. The most appropriate place for an in-tray is on your work desk and next to your computer, which also acts as the admin hub of the home. Rather than leave potentially sensitive papers scattered throughout the home, by keeping everything in one place you're less likely to forget to pay a bill or RSVP to an invite.

FILE

First off, request paperless billing for whatever you can. As most things are available digitally, there really isn't much need to hold on to statements and bills. If you can download a bank statement via online banking, shred the paper original rather than file it. For documents relating to tax, insurance, vehicles and medical records, you may have to hold on to paperwork for a while, so choose a small but strong waterproof/fireproof file box or an accordion file so that you won't be tempted to hold on to too many documents, but those important ones will be protected. Add labels to the different sections of the filing system so everything is clearly marked. Within the sections of the file, place the newest paperwork at the front. When filing something like a vehicle MOT certificate, place the current year's certificate at the front and then remove and shred the out-of-date certificate from the back.

With the exception of birth certificates, marriage licences, property deeds, wills and other important legal documents, never store beyond seven years. Tax inspectors may ask to review paperwork from the last seven years, but for everything else three years is usually plenty long enough. Warranties can be kept for the life of the product, after that they are irrelevant.

ARCHIVE

As with other categories, sentimental items that fall into paperwork are often the hardest to sort. Tickets, leaflets, photos, cards, drawings, but also clippings, articles, recipes, etc. Ask yourself why you are holding on to these things. Sometimes it will be obvious – that an item brings back a happy or important memory that you want to hold on to. Otherwise, it could be an article to read, a recipe to try or an inspiration photo for redecorating. For true sentimental items, consider a memory box, but regularly re-evaluate to make sure that everything is deserving of its place in there. For everything else, let it go. If you haven't tried that recipe by now, are you

'DO A DIGITAL DETOX SO THAT YOUR MAIL DOESN'T PILE UP. AND MAKE THE SHIFT TO GO ONLINE SO THAT IT GIVES YOU SPACE BACK IN YOUR HOME OFFICE AND YOU HAVE A CLEAR DESK WITHOUT MOUNDS OF PAPERWORK EVERYWHERE.'

DILLY

really going to? Most articles can now be read online on the publication's website. That coupon has probably now expired.

HOW TO MINIMISE PAPERWORK

✳ **Invest in a scanner** – most home printers have a scanner function or there are apps you can put onto your smartphone that act as a scanner. Make a quick scan of receipts, invoices and notes that you want to retain for reference but don't need a physical copy of. This way they don't take up physical space, only digital space. (To keep the carbon footprint of storing data as low as possible, put the scans on a USB stick and store it in a drawer, then from time to time, audit this digital archive and delete scans no longer needed.)

✳ **Declutter papers regularly** – once a bill is paid, do you need to keep it for your records or can you shred and recycle it? If you file a tax return, be aware that you will need to keep hold of all records relating to that tax return for seven years after submission just in case HMRC call you up for any further checks. So, keep seven years of financial records and three years of anything else.

✳ **Unsubscribe** – whenever you can, unsubscribe from company mailing lists so that you will no longer receive both junk emails and junk mail, especially bulky mail-order catalogues that consume a lot of paper. An added bonus is that you won't be lured into purchasing those so-called great deals, which nine times out of ten aren't so great or they're things that you don't really need.

SYSTEMISE > THE SPARE ROOM, LOFT, GARAGE AND OTHER SPACES

A loft, garage or any other type of storage space is an incredible luxury. Such a space can be really useful, but it can also be a real danger. If you start to shove stuff in there without any system, it can quickly become a cluttered 'room of doom' that's full of everything and anything. And you'll never be able to get in there and find what you need, so you'll never use any of that stuff. The primary objective for these types of spaces is to stop them from becoming a dumping ground for all manner of clutter. The best way to do this is to give every space a purpose so that it has a structure and a system, so there is no such thing as a 'spare' room.

REAL LIFE INSPO

Aimee and Stuart moved out of a flat and into a house with a garage. After four years in their current house, the garage was still full of the untouched, unpacked boxes of possessions they boxed up and moved from the flat. This was a classic case of 'out of sight, out of mind'. Despite their best intentions to tackle the boxes, it kept being put off. Aimee admitted that they often said, 'We'll do that next weekend,' and then next weekend turned into next year. As this stuff had been untouched in boxes for four years, and Aimee and Stuart had not seen it, missed it, wanted it or needed it, it was time to let it go.'

'THE TERM "SPARE ROOM" MAKES ME SHUDDER. IT MAKES NO SENSE TO ME TO HAVE A ROOM IN THE HOUSE THAT DOESN'T HAVE A PURPOSE. IF IT DOESN'T HAVE A LABEL — WHETHER THAT BE A PLAYROOM, A GYM, A GUEST ROOM, WHATEVER IT IS — IT JUST BECOMES A JUNK ROOM.'

STACEY

STORAGE

When storing possessions in a loft, garage or other space, put everything into stackable, see-through plastic boxes. When the box is see-through, it makes it so much easier to tell what is in each box. But label things too so that you don't have to disturb everything to find that one possession.

SYSTEMISE > SENTIMENTAL ITEMS

We all have a certain amount of possessions that mean something to us and that we don't want to part with, which is actually something to be celebrated. These cherished objects make a space feel homely and reflect who we are. Without family photos, mementos and other inherited pieces, a home may feel a little soulless. The trick is not to let them get out of control and take over a space, but to display these cherished items properly and allow them to breathe.

Rather than storing boxes and boxes of photographs that you rarely look at, sort through any prints to filter out the bad ones from the good ones. If the shot is blurred or there's a finger in front of the lens, then it can probably go. And if there are lots of similar frames, then choose just the best one. If you don't have a digital copy, keep the original print along with the negative, but if the photo exists digitally, then ask yourself whether it's worth keeping the print too. Once you've edited the prints down to a manageable selection, either display them or store them in labelled albums. It's generally a good idea to organise the photos by year and event, such as Christmas 2023 and Stacey and Joe's wedding. **The golden rule is:** display those photographs that you cherish and store in albums any prints that you cannot display.

HERO PRODUCT: BOX FRAMES

Box frames are perfect for displaying three-dimensional items, such as precious jewellery or other inherited items. For example, Tony inherited his late father's hammer, which was very precious to him but it had been lost in the chaos of clutter. Now that it is displayed in a box frame against a wooden backing board, he'll never lose that hammer again.

HOW TO UPCYCLE SENTIMENTAL ITEMS

Baby items are often kept as keepsakes, even though they no longer serve a purpose, so try to think of ways in which they can be repurposed to make something else.

REAL LIFE INSPO

All of the muslins that Tash had held on to from when Jacob, Elijah, Grace and Thea were babies were trimmed into squares and stitched together to make a memory quilt that now acts as a throw on Tash and Lawrence's bed. Now their babies will forever be close. Similarly, some of the 364 babygrows that Chloe had kept from when her two daughters were young, were cut up and made into a string of scalloped bunting to decorate their room. Find your own ways of holding on to memories that also makes space for future memories.

STORING GREETINGS CARDS

Many people can fall into the habit of keeping every greetings card they receive, but you should only ever hold on to the ones that really mean something to you and spark emotion. To store them efficiently, make them into 'books' for each occasion. Take the largest card, open it out and layer inside all the other cards, working downwards in size order. Once all the cards are in a stack, punch two holes in the back side of the cards near to the crease and thread a length of ribbon that is then tied to hold the book together.

MAKING A MEMORY BOX

There's no set way to make or store a memory box: those possessions that spark memories are personal to you and it's up to you what you keep. You may want to have one memory box for each child or for each relationship. The size of the box will also depend on what you might keep, but it's good to use an attractive box with a lid, especially if you're going to have it on display. Depending on how deeply you feel about sentimental items, you may want to keep them on display in a place where they can easily be accessed so that you can leaf through them whenever you feel the need and new items can be added. Or, if you know that you'll only ever look through the box very occasionally and are unlikely to add more to it, then the box can be stored away in the loft or another more remote space to make room for other items.

'NOW I HAVE A CONSTANT LEVEL OF HAPPINESS, WHEREAS BEFORE I HAD A CONSTANT LEVEL OF STRESS.'

CHLOE, SERIES THREE

Step Three:
Systemise Checklist

---

1. MAKE SURE EVERY SPACE HAS A CLEAR FUNCTION, ZONING AREAS WITHIN ROOMS IF NECESSARY.

2. CONSIDER WHERE THE FURNITURE IS PLACED, ORGANISING IT SO IT MAKES THE MOST SENSE.

3. MAXIMISE ALL THE AVAILABLE STORAGE AND SNEAK IN SOME EXTRA WHERE POSSIBLE.

4. ARRANGE YOUR 'KEEP' ITEMS IN THEIR DESIGNATED SPACE, LABELLING CUPBOARDS, DRAWERS AND CONTAINERS TO MAKE THINGS SUPER CLEAR.

5. GET ALL THE FAMILY SIGNED UP TO FOLLOW THE NEW SYSTEMS, SO THIS IS A FRESH NEW START FOR EVERYONE.

Welcome to your brand-new home! With less clutter, more storage and some systems in place, we hope that this is now a place where you will feel relaxed and happy. And with less time spent tidying and cleaning, it will give you more time to do the things you love with those you love the most.

STAY
ORGANISED

As you've all done such an amazing job in sorting your stuff, letting go of things and organising your home, it would be a real shame to let any clutter creep back in. Now that the hard work has been done and you've experienced the joy of living with less mess, you'll feel more motivated to keep on top of everything. Staying organised is a case of being restrained in what you buy or bring into the home, decluttering regularly to control the chaos and following all those systems for neatly storing stuff away. To keep on top of things and not fall back into old habits, there are a few key rules for shopping, decluttering and cleaning that are good to stick to:

Shopping rules

1. BUY NOTHING FOR A FULL MONTH

After your epic declutter, set your family the challenge not to buy anything new for one month other than the absolute essentials, like fresh foods (although you will probably have enough in the fridge, freezer and cupboards to keep you going for a while). Psychologists maintain that it takes just 21 days to ditch old habits and form new ones, so after one month, you should have broken the habit of making impulse purchases and understand that saving money and space in your home by not shopping can give you just as much of a buzz.

2. NEVER BUY BLIND

Always shop with a list and buy only what you need. If you make meal plans and keep an inventory of what's in the freezer and fridge, then you'll avoid wasting money on food you don't need or items that go out of date before they can be eaten. And always use up a product before buying another similar one, even if the new purchase promises to change your life – it rarely does!

3. STOP MAKING IMPULSE PURCHASES

Weigh up what's more important – the bargain buy or the storage space that it's going to take up. Those tempting offers in the middle aisle might seem too good to be true, but is it really a bargain if you're never going to use it? Consider what's more valuable to you: a cheap item that you may only use once or the space that would be freed up if it wasn't there.

REAL LIFE INSPO

When we met Stuart and Roydel, both in series two, they were addicted to special buys, but the goods remained in their boxes unused. For both of them, finding a bargain had become a hobby in itself, almost irrespective of what the item was. We've all fallen for it – you go in for a carton of milk and you end up coming out with a chainsaw! However, those things that you believe will give you the perfect home actually end up being detrimental to home life because they fill up the space.

4. RENT OR BORROW INSTEAD

If you're only going to use or wear something once, consider renting or borrowing the item instead of spending money on something new. Useful libraries of things, where you can borrow DIY tools, are popping up all over the country and there are lots of dress agencies, both on the high street and online, that will rent you an outfit for a special event.

5. GIFT EXPERIENCES, NOT THINGS

The expectation is to always give an object as a gift, but often there is nothing that anyone really needs. Children especially have loads of clothes, books and toys, so giving them another one as a present is just adding to the pile. Think about giving an experience to someone instead, that way you'll get to spend time together and make memories.

6. ONLY MAKE CONSIDERED PURCHASES

To make sure you only buy those things that you need and will use, whenever you're tempted into buying something new, pause and ask yourself these crucial questions to find out whether you really need to make that purchase:

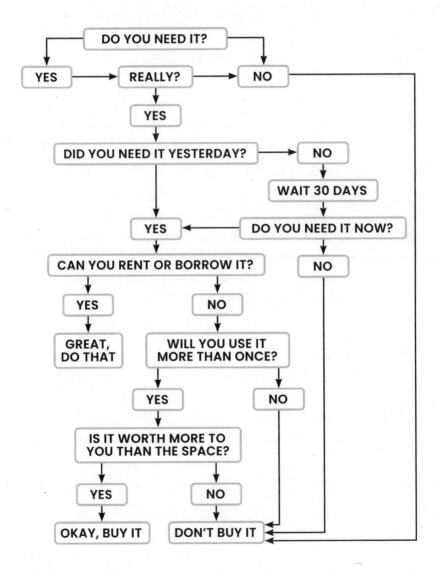

7. DO NOT CHECKOUT IMMEDIATELY

If you do spot something you need or love online, add it to your virtual shopping basket but do not checkout. Leave it there for at least seven days and if you find yourself being drawn back to it and you definitely need it, will use it and love it, then make a considered purchase rather than an impulse purchase. Often retailers send a discount code if you show interest in an item but leave it in the shopping basket without purchasing, so it can pay to play the waiting game.

8. IMPLEMENT A ONE-IN, ONE-OUT POLICY

Offset any new purchase by offloading an old one. If you buy new bath towels, for example, then that should be because your existing ones have worn out, so recycle the old ones promptly rather than hanging on to them 'just in case'. The same goes for any clothes and accessories. If you buy a new jumper, look at a jumper that you haven't worn for ages and ask yourself 'Can that one now go?' And when it comes to books, once you've read a novel, be honest about whether you'll ever want to read it again. It's far more satisfying to pass the book on to a friend and then you can discuss your thoughts on the novel together.

'WHEN YOU'VE GOT AN EMOTIONAL ATTACHMENT TO A TOY, BUT YOUR CHILDREN HAVE GROWN OUT OF IT, IT'S ALMOST LIKE GRIEF BECAUSE YOU KNOW THAT PERIOD OF TIME WITH YOUR CHILD IS GONE. SO MANY TIMES I'VE HELD ON TO THINGS AND THEN I'VE GOT THEM OUT OF THE MEMORY BOX AND SAID, "HERE'S THAT STONE YOU PICKED UP FIVE YEARS AGO," AND THE KIDS HAVE JUST GONE "HUH?"'

STACEY

Decluttering rules

1. MAKE A DATE TO DECLUTTER

You need to regularly revisit what you're keeping in your home and reassess whether it's now time to let go of something, Every six months, put a date in your diary to review all those items that aren't used on a weekly basis. How you feel about your possessions will change over time and what felt essential to hold on to last year may seem less crucial as time passes and your attachment wanes. If you can have decluttering moments throughout the rest of your life, then you won't ever go back to the point of overwhelming clutter.

2. DO THE HANGER EDIT

This is a simple system for identifying just how many of your clothes you actually wear each month. At the start of the month, make sure all the hooks of every hanger are facing in the same direction. Whenever you wear something, when you rehang it in the wardrobe, turn the hook of the hanger to face in the opposite direction (but if you wear it twice, don't turn the hanger back again). At the end of each month, you can easily tell which clothes you've worn by the direction the hanger hook is facing. Edit those clothes that are unworn at the end of the month and let go of anything that you haven't worn and don't love or need.

3. KEEP A DONATION BASKET IN THE BOTTOM OF THE WARDROBE

Follow Dilly's tip to maintain a clutter-free capsule wardrobe and place a basket in the bottom of the wardrobe, then drop in any clothes that you didn't enjoy wearing or decide you no longer like. This is something that every family member can easily do. At the end of each month, either sell or donate these garments. Once you've created the perfect capsule wardrobe, it's fine to tweak and refresh it with new items from time to time, but don't lose the essence of having a slimmed-down, flexible wardrobe of coordinating quality pieces.

4. STICK TO YOUR PAPERWORK PROTOCOL

Tackle every bit of paper as soon as it arrives. When a mail-order catalogue lands on the doormat, look at it straight away. If there's nothing of interest to you, then immediately unsubscribe and recycle it. When a note arrives home in the school satchel, read it, sign it and send it back. When those brown envelopes turn up, open them immediately and action payment by either paying straight away or scheduling payment (if you need to budget), so you can move the bill straight from the action pile to be filed. And then request paperless billing for the future.

5. REMEMBER YOUR WHY

There was a powerful reason why you all embarked on this strip, sort and systemise process (see page 18). So, whenever things feel tough, take a moment to reflect on that reason why and focus on the benefits that staying organised brings to your family life.

6. GIVING FEELS GOOD

Remind yourself that for every possession that you donate, someone else will get the pleasure of it in their lives.

Organisation and cleaning rules

1. SHARE THE RESPONSIBILITY

One person shouldn't feel like they have to do it all on their own. By now, every household member should understand the systems and how the house should run. By sorting their own stuff, everyone will have seen how they contributed to the problem but also understand how they're part of the solution. Achieving and maintaining an organised home is a team effort.

2. CREATE A CHIPPING-IN CHART

Because keeping the home organised is not a solo task and everyone needs to play their part, make a chipping-in chart with a rota for chores around the house (see the housework checklist on page 227). Under each family member's name, write a list of daily tasks for them to complete on a specific day so that everyone knows what they're expected to do each week. As the saying goes, 'Many hands make light work.'

3. DIP INTO THE TO-DO JAR

For less-frequent chores that don't need to be done each day, keep a to-do jar that everyone dips into each week or month. Write these individual tasks on wooden lolly sticks that are kept in a jar. Each member of the family takes a lucky dip and then has to carry out the chore written on the lolly stick.

4. HAVE A HOUSEWORK CHECKLIST

Keeping a checklist of daily, weekly, monthly and even yearly tasks means that all those cleaning chores are more likely to be completed. Yes, this is a long list, which looks a bit daunting when written down, but many of these tasks take mere minutes and can be shared amongst all the members of the household.

'I JUST DON'T SEE WHY AN ENTIRE FAMILY CAN'T GET INVOLVED IN ALL OF THE CHORES. MOST PEOPLE ARE WORKING, AND THEN THEY'RE TRYING TO RUN A HOUSE ... IF PEOPLE DON'T CHIP IN AND DO THEIR BIT, THEN IT BECOMES IMPOSSIBLE, WHICH MAKES LIFE HARD FOR EVERYBODY.'

STACEY

'A HOUSE DOESN'T RUN ITSELF. BY HAVING A ROTA OR A SCHEDULE, EACH MEMBER OF THE FAMILY CAN BE ASSIGNED A TASK. EVERYONE CAN NOW TAKE PART IN HELPING OUT AROUND THE HOUSE!

DILLY

The ideal housework checklist

||| DAILY TASKS

- ❏ MAKE YOUR BED AS SOON AS YOU GET UP
- ❏ PLACE ANY DIRTY CLOTHES DIRECTLY INTO THE LAUNDRY BASKET
- ❏ LOAD DIRTY ITEMS STRAIGHT INTO THE DISHWASHER OR SINK
- ❏ CLEAR ALL SURFACES OF CLUTTER AT THE END OF EACH DAY
- ❏ WIPE DOWN ALL COUNTERTOPS
- ❏ RETURN USED ITEMS TO THEIR DESIGNATED PLACE
- ❏ PLUMP ALL THE SOFA CUSHIONS
- ❏ SORT ANY MAIL, CATALOGUES AND OTHER PAPERWORK AS THEY ARRIVE AND TAKE IMMEDIATE ACTION
- ❏ EMPTY ANY WASTE BINS

||| WEEKLY TASKS

- ❏ CHANGE YOUR BED LINEN AND LAUNDER THE USED SET

- ❏ LAUNDER ALL DIRTY CLOTHES

- ❏ PUT AWAY ANY LAUNDERED CLOTHES IN THE CORRECT PLACE

- ❏ WIPE DOWN APPLIANCES

- ❏ CLEAN THE DISHWASHER FILTER

- ❏ STEAM—CLEAN YOUR MICROWAVE WITH LEMON WATER

- ❏ UNSCREW THE KITCHEN PLUGHOLE AND THOROUGHLY CLEAN TO PREVENT BLOCKAGES

- ❏ DUST AND POLISH WOODEN FURNITURE AND SHELVING

- ❏ VACUUM OR SWEEP FLOORS, CARPETS AND RUGS (ESPECIALLY IF YOU HAVE PETS)

❏ WASH OR STEAM—CLEAN HARD FLOORS
(ESPECIALLY IF YOU HAVE PETS)

❏ SCRUB THE TOILET, BATH, SINK AND SHOWER

❏ CLEAN MIRRORS

❏ PUT OUT THE RUBBISH AND PUT OUT THE
RECYCLING FOR COLLECTION

||| **MONTHLY**

- ❏ CLEAN AND REORGANISE THE FRIDGE
- ❏ DEEP CLEAN THE OVEN
- ❏ CLEAN INSIDE THE KITCHEN CABINETS
- ❏ CLEAN ALL THE WINDOWS
- ❏ WIPE DOWN DOORKNOBS, SWITCH PLATES AND LIGHT SWITCHES TO REMOVE FINGERMARKS
- ❏ CHECK YOUR SMOKE DETECTORS ARE WORKING AND CHANGE THE BATTERIES, IF NECESSARY
- ❏ DISINFECT ALL WASTE BINS
- ❏ DONATE ANY SURPLUS FOOD ITEMS THAT YOU WON'T GET THROUGH TO A FOOD BANK
- ❏ SELL, DONATE OR RECYCLE ANY UNWORN OR UNWANTED CLOTHES FROM THE WARDROBE BASKETS
- ❏ ROTATE THE KIDS' TOYS TO KEEP THEM INTERESTED

||| SIX-MONTHLY

- ❏ ROTATE YOUR SEASONAL CLOTHES AND PACK AWAY ANY WINTER ITEMS DURING SUMMER OR SUMMER ITEMS DURING WINTER

- ❏ AIR DUVETS, BLANKETS AND THROWS, AND DRY–CLEAN IF NECESSARY

- ❏ SELL, DONATE OR RECYCLE ANY KIDS' TOYS THAT ARE NO LONGER PLAYED WITH

- ❏ REASSESS ANY POSSESSIONS THAT AREN'T USED WEEKLY TO CHECK YOU WANT TO KEEP HOLD OF THEM

⦀ YEARLY

- ❑ CHECK BED LINENS AND REPLACE WORN SETS, IF NECESSARY

- ❑ CHECK TOWELS AND REPLACE WORN ONES, IF NECESSARY

- ❑ CHECK CROCKERY, GLASSWARE AND CUTLERY, LETTING GO OF ANY EXCESS OR BROKEN PIECES

- ❑ SHRED AND RECYCLE ANY EXPIRED PAPERWORK (YOU ONLY NEED TO KEEP THE PREVIOUS SEVEN YEARS FOR TAX RECORDS AND THREE YEARS FOR ANYTHING ELSE)

'IT'S ALLOWED US TO SPEND A LOT MORE TIME WITH EACH OTHER, AND THAT WAS THE WHOLE POINT OF GOING THROUGH THIS PROCESS. I ABSOLUTELY FEEL LIKE WE'VE GOT OUR FOREVER HOME NOW.'

CHARLIE, SERIES FOUR

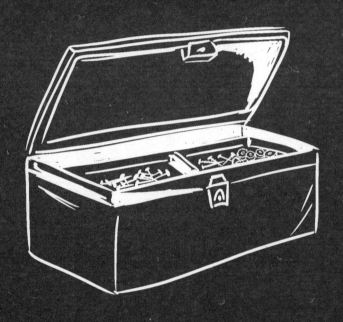

IDEAS FOR EXTRA STORAGE AND UPCYCLING

Storage is essential in every home, and no one ever feels as though they have enough. Whenever we visit a family, the first things we look for are cost-effective ways to increase the amount of available storage space and make the most of what's already there. Rob never fails to come up with genius ideas for creating storage where there was previously none or flexible space-saving furniture. And because Stacey loves to get her craft on and reuse whatever she can in the most sustainable way possible, we upcycle whatever existing furniture and homeware that we can breathe new life into. We aim never to send decent items to landfill, so we're always looking for ways to renovate and repurpose what a family already owns – it's better for their pocket and for the planet. Happy days, money saved.

Upcycling

PAINT TO PERFECTION

One of the simplest ways to upcycle
furniture is to apply a coat of paint. Using one
key colour can unify a room scheme and marry
up disparate styles of furniture, while a range of tones
can add highlights and extra interest.

✳ Using a single shade of paint is a smart way of tying a
number of different pieces of furniture together to make
a more cohesive decorative scheme. Rather than incur
the unnecessary expense of replacing wardrobes and
chests of drawers, at Sue's home in series two we worked
with only the pieces of furniture that she already owned
to revamp her bedroom. Rob and the team painted a
number of assorted units in the same delicate tone of
pale blue, along with using a pretty vinyl wrap in a floral
design, to instantly elevate the room.

✳ Using up tester pots of paint in different shades is a thrifty
way of upcycling furniture. Stacey gave a fresh look to
a chest of drawers found in Cherelle and Tony's house
by painting each of the five drawers in a different shade
from the same column of the paint chart used on the
bedroom walls, so that every colour in the space worked
together as they're from the same tonal range. Stacey
created a stunning ombre paint effect that moved from
light on the top drawer to dark on the bottom drawer.
If you do the same, it's important to change the roller

between each paint colour. And if you're painting a piece of furniture for a child's room, use wipeable paint to keep it looking its best.

✳ Forget ripping out your kitchen, or even replacing the door and drawer fronts, as that can be one of the most expensive things you can do in your home. Updating units with a bit of paint is such an amazing way to give an entire kitchen a brand-new feel for a fraction of the price of a new kitchen. That's exactly what Stacey did in Claire's utility room in series three, so that the whole room felt refreshed and is now a calm, organised space so that even her five boys can get involved in the cleaning of the house. Just remember to remove or tape up the handles before painting any unit doors and drawers. And when a door has quite intricate details, start with a brush to get the paint right into the grooves. Once you've got all your tricky corners done, it's roller time. Apply a primer or sealer and then two or three coats of eggshell paint for the best coverage.

HERO PRODUCT: STICK—ON VINYL

This clever sticky-back vinyl sheeting is now available in so many colours and patterns. You can use it to cover furniture, kitchen units, countertops and even appliances for an instant change. You can transform pieces of furniture, like a chest of drawers, with it along with new handles. We transformed a chest of drawers for a kid's room using Dalmatian spots.

BEADING MAKES EVERYTHING BETTER

Adding a strip of beading, or bead moulding, is a way of elevating basic or flatpack furniture so that it instantly looks more expensive.

✳ In series two, we decided that Aimee and Stuart's old wardrobe was too small and just not practical, so we swapped it for a larger wardrobe with plain white doors. But to make it look a "little bit more posh", Stacey added strips of beading to give this basic piece of furniture a more antique and expensive look. She cut the strips to size using mitre scissors to create a 45-degree angle at the end of each strip, so they came together neatly at the corners. Stacey then used wood glue to fix the strips of beading in place, but you could also use a nail gun.

✳ Mirrored wardrobe doors can feel a bit 1980s, but adding painted MDF strips to create a panelled effect is an affordable way to bring them bang up to date. That's exactly what we did in the master bedroom at Char and Dan's house, in series two, to modernise the fitted wardrobes in their rented home. Three horizontal strips of MDF painted in a chic slate grey made up a panel effect and tied in with the painted surround.

GET INTO THE GROOVE

Another way to elevate a space and tie together various elements is to clad walls or furniture in tongue-and-groove boards. Because you can buy packs of these boards pre-cut, it's a simple effect that you can achieve yourself at home without calling in a carpenter.

✳ In series three, we used lots of our favourite tricks to make Lianne and Andy's hallway both a functional and beautiful space. Stacey clad the walls of the long narrow hallway with slot-together tongue-and-groove boards, from the skirting to three-quarters of the way up the wall. We then wallpapered the top quarter of the wall with a pretty pattern of leaves and acorns, which we also took over the ceiling for a wrap-around effect. Rob then made seating benches from basic flat-pack furniture to provide the family with tonnes of shoe storage that was then elevated with identical tongue-and-groove boards to tie in with the walls. Picking up on the green shades in the wallpaper leaf pattern, all the woodwork and furniture were painted in the same soft sage green.

✳ Stacey created a feature wall in Toyah and Ron's bedroom with a modern take on wood-clad walls using elegant, yet inexpensive, thin battens. She sanded them down to ensure all edges were smooth, then stained each one so that it looked like oak. Stacey fixed each batten to the wall using an air-compress staple gun for ease, but you could easily use nails. To make sure the gaps between each upright batten were the same, Stacey used a block of wood as a spacer and a spirit level.

FIRE UP A FOCAL POINT

Even if you don't have a working chimney, a decorative fireplace provides a simple way to add character and an attractive focal point to a living room.

✳ While we were exploring Julia and Dan's home in series two, we found a fireplace surround in their garden that had never been fitted. It only needed sanding and painting before it could be fitted to the wall, but then there was the question of what should go inside the opening in place of an actual fire. Stacey came up with the idea of a log stack, so she took some basic logs in a range of thicknesses and then sliced them into 5cm-thick rounds. If you do the same, it's really important to wear protective goggles, gloves and a mask when cutting wood with a power saw. Mixing and matching the different sizes, those log rounds were then glued to a panel of MDF cut to fit the opening before Stacey and the team mounted the fireplace on the wall over the panel of logs. Whatever you do, just <u>don't try to light the fire</u>.

FROM COT TO POT RACK

Before you recycle anything you no longer need, pause for just a moment to think whether it could be repurposed for another function.

* For Daniela and Tim's kitchen, Rob took the baby cot they no longer needed (as their youngest daughter was actually seven) and transformed one of the sides into a hanging rack for their pots and pans. He drilled holes that were 10cm apart all along the bars of the cot and added lengths of chain fixed to each corner. The new rack was then hung from a secure hook in the ceiling and individual butcher's hooks were slotted into the drilled holes to create places to hang the pots and pans by their handles. Dilly's tip here is to hang the pots in size order, from the largest to the smallest.

* In series three, Stacey jumped on the 'breadside table' bandwagon. Following this popular trend that's all over social media, she took two classic bread bins, turned them on their sides so their flat bottoms were placed together, then bolted them together by screwing on some short table legs. Take a slice of inspiration from Stacey and make your own breadside table.

* At Sue's house, in series two, her bed was lacking a headboard. For a quick fix, Stacey took a wooden curtain pole that she fixed to the wall at just the right height above Sue's bed and then tied two outdoor seating cushions to the pole so that they hung down to make a soft, padded headboard. It's a really cost-effective way of creating a comfy headboard that makes a perfect spot to recline.

Extra storage

 HIDDEN GEMS

Instead of adding another piece of furniture to a space, look to see whether there are any existing areas currently not being used for storage that could be put to work. Rob has created invaluable extra storage in some surprising places.

✳ For Steph and her three daughters, who all share a bathroom, Rob made extra storage hidden behind the panel around the bath. With push-close panels, each family member now has their own section for bathroom products that sit in the cavity between the bath panel and the actual bowl of the bathtub. This gave them more storage but without taking anything away from the room at all. If you're making any bespoke storage in the bathroom, use moisture-resistant MDF, which is also known as green MDF.

✳ For Tash, Lawrence and their four kids, Rob came up with a clever shoe storage solution by creating pull-out drawers hidden in the stairs, so the family won't need to hunt for lost shoes ever again. Using a template, Rob made shallow drawer boxes to fit the stairs and then cut openings in the risers that each drawer box was slotted into. He then used side-mounted drawer runners to hold the pull-out drawers in place. While it's best to make the drawer box and pull-out drawer from cheap plywood, you can use a more expensive material for the visible drawer front. Alternatively, you could turn the tread of each step into a lift-up lid so the cavity below can be accessed from above. You might want to allocate one drawer per family member so that everyone has their own space, or you may prefer to dedicate one drawer to shoes and then use another drawer for dog leads, umbrellas or other everyday items that are best kept in the hallway.

PUT A LID ON IT

Rather than a regular coffee table or seating bench, one with a lift-up lid or slide-open top can give a game-changing amount of extra storage space.

✳ Why have a table with a straightforward top when it can open up to reveal some hidden storage? In more than one family home, Rob has transformed a coffee table or other unit into a flexible piece of furniture with space beneath for storing books and other items out of sight. Venicia, Elisha and their family love to cosy up under blankets when watching TV, so the coffee table now doubles as storage for blankets.

✳   Built-in banquet seating or a freestanding seating
bench is the perfect place for smart storage. For Chloe
and Tom, who have a collection of board games, Rob
built some bespoke banquet seating in their dining
zone. Underneath the seating cushions, the lift-up lids
of the bench give them access to loads more storage.
Rob also fitted pockets to the underside of the lid of
the bench to slide in their most-used games so they'll
always be easily accessible.

||| DROP IT DOWN

Flexible furniture that can be dropped down or folded out
and then packed away neatly when not in use can be the
most sensible use of space when it's at a premium. This can
be a drop-down bed in a home office, a fold-away dining
table in a multifunctional living space or a pull-out work desk
in a bedroom.

✳   Rob combined a toy storage unit together with a
retractable dining table for Craig in series four to give
him and his girls somewhere to gather together for
meals, but also for Merywen and Wren to paint and
play. What acts as the surface of the storage unit when
it's up against the wall then slides across and pivots
90 degrees before being locked into position. Once the
tabletop swings out into the room, it makes a practical
large table, but once it's back over the unit, it frees up the
room for the kids' playtime.

'A REALLY COMMON MISTAKE THAT PEOPLE MAKE IS TO BUY FURNITURE THAT'S FAR TOO BIG FOR THEIR HOME. IT LOOKS GREAT THERE ON THE SHOP FLOOR, BUT THAT DOESN'T MEAN IT'S GOING TO LOOK GOOD IN YOUR HOUSE.'

ROB

✳ At Charlie and Keith's house, their old nursery was repurposed as an office for Keith to work from home, away from other distractions. Rob fitted a sleek unit to one wall that contained a pull-down bed, which can be used when occasional guests come to stay. When the bed is packed away, the unit doesn't take up very much space at all but gives them flexible options.

HERO PRODUCT: CASTORS

Fitting castors to furniture means that the piece can be effortlessly moved around. Rob put castors on the legs of an oak table he found in a junkyard to make a crafting station for Lianne in series three. When it's not in use, the unit can be wheeled easily into the corner of the room whenever husband Andy wants to use his gym equipment. And for extra storage in Sydnie's bedroom, whom we met in series one, Stacey popped a castor in each corner of some spare wardrobe drawers to make under-bed storage that can easily be wheeled out.

 CUT DOWN TO SIZE

You'd be surprised how often people try to squeeze oversized furniture into their homes that is just too large for the room and prevents the space from flowing. But you don't always need to ditch that table, unit or wardrobe as good wooden furniture can be adapted.

* Tash and Lawrence thought a three-door wardrobe seemed like a good idea for storing their mountain of clothes, but after letting go of so many unworn garments during the sort stage, there was simply no need for such a large lump of furniture in the room. Rob carefully cut down the wardrobe to reduce it from three doors to two doors. To do this, he took the wardrobe apart before cutting down and reassembling the panels to make sure that it looked like it was always intended to be a two-door wardrobe.

* For Toyah and Ron's home, in series two, Rob took their existing kitchen table that didn't fit the shape and reinvented it as a coffee table. He did this by cutting the legs down to take it from waist height to knee height, then also by shaving bits off the tabletop to turn a circle into an oval shape.

* Instead of two separate cabin beds that took up almost all of the space in Aria and Nerea's shared bedroom, Rob repurposed them to make bespoke bunk beds that are actually a bunk-bed house. Rob added a pitched roof with scalloped eaves and window frames with flower boxes to make something quite unique. The girls now have much more free floor space that they can play on as well as a really fun place to sleep.

RESOURCES

 SELL, DONATE, RECYCLE

Once you've selected those items that you're going to keep, everything else should be either sold, donated or recycled. Which of these options you choose will depend on the condition of the item and what is the most suitable outcome. Here are just some of the organisations that can help you make responsible choices for those possessions you are no longer keeping:

SELL

Nowadays, there are so many online auction sites and apps that make it super easy to sell the stuff that you no longer want. Some of the most popular are eBay, Facebook Marketplace, Shpock, Vinted, Gumtree and Nextdoor. And don't forget about car boot sales. It might mean getting up extra early, but a car boot sale is a great way to shift a lot of stuff in one morning.

DONATE

If you'd rather donate an item instead of selling it, whatever that item is, it must be in a good, saleable condition.

Don't treat any charity shop as a dumping ground as charities do get charged for taking unsuitable items away. Before you lug all your donations over to the shop, it's a good idea to check that they are accepting donations that day as they can be full. Some also offer a collection service, so they may pick up from your home – it's always worth checking. There are also quite a few online sites where you can do someone else a good turn and offer your stuff for free, such as Freecycle, Freegle and Trash Nothing (other companies are available). In return, they will collect from your address.

RECYCLE

Once you've exhausted the sell and donate options, it may be that recycling an item is the most appropriate outcome, particularly when it is broken or unusable. If you're unsure how to recycle any specific item, have a google or visit sites such as www.gov.uk/recycling-collections or recyclenow.com.

 ## SUPPORT ORGANISATIONS

Decluttering is best done when you're in the right headspace. Due to the clutter, your home may well have been getting you down, which can cause feelings of stress, frustration and hopelessness. However, if you're experiencing deeper issues surrounding your mental health, seek advice from a medical professional, starting with your GP. They can help you understand what lies behind any unhappiness – for example, the loss of a loved one – and get you the help that you need.

THERAPY FOR BETTER MENTAL HEALTH

Betterhelp (betterhelp.com) can link you to an appropriate therapist in your local area. You can also find helpful resources at Mind (mind.org.uk), Young Minds (youngminds.org.uk), CAMHS (www.oxfordhealth.charity), NHS (nhs.uk/nhs-services/mental-health-services) and BBC Action Line (www.bbc.co.uk/actionline).

COUNSELLING FOR BEREAVEMENT

AtaLoss (ataloss.org), Cruse (cruse.org.uk), Marie Curie (mariecurie.org.uk) and Sue Ryder (sueryder.org) all offer bereavement and grief counselling. You can find a list of more organisations on BBC Action Line (www.bbc.co.uk/actionline).

TREATMENT FOR HOARDING DISORDER

Mind (mind.org.uk) and Hoarding Disorders UK (hoardingdisordersuk.org) have helpful information on their website for treating hoarding disorder.

INDEX

access, ease of 34
accessories 94–5, 96, 148
aprons, folding 182–3
artwork 193–4

baby items 154–5, 207, 243
bathrooms 61–4, 98–9, 157–65, 244
battens 241
batteries 110
beading 240
bed linen 96, 104–5, 187–91, 232
bedrooms 243
    cleaning 61
    kids' 96, 150–6, 249
    master 94–6, 131–49
    occasional 248
benches 245–6
bereavement 21, 28–9, 252
best-before dates 103–4
bicarbonate of soda 61–5, 67, 69–70
bins, cleaning 67
biro marks 68
blankets 96, 104–5, 245
blinds, cleaning 57–8
blood sugar levels 41
board games 193, 246
books 86, 106–7, 109, 217, 219, 245
borrowing 25, 217
box frames 24, 131, 207
boxer shorts 144–5
'breadside tables' 243
broken items 50

caddies 186–7
car boot sales 92
carpets 59, 60, 70
carrier bags 178
castors 248
CDs 106, 107, 195
ceilings 57, 62, 65
chalkboards 178, 197
change, resistance to 39
chests of drawers 238–9
chipping-in charts 224
chunking tasks 20

cladding 241
cleaning 54–72
    checklists 224, 227–9
    kit 54–5
    as shared responsibility 223–6
    and staying organised 215, 223–32
    top down approach to 58
cleaning pads, DIY 67
cleaning products 61–5, 67, 69–71, 104, 186–7
cleaning wipes, eco-friendly 71
clothes hangers 132–3, 136, 221
    valet hangers 149
clothes moths 60
clothing 50
    buying rules 217, 219
    donation baskets 222
    dot system 156
    file folding 136–47, 153–5
    hanger edit 221
    hanging 81, 95, 133–6
    holding onto 19, 27
    kids' 153–6
    renting/borrowing 217
    seasonal 149
    sorting 81, 84, 94–6
    starting with 84
    storage 133–49, 153–6
    worn 149
    see also wardrobes
clutter
    impact of 15, 16, 31
    limiting 86
    why we hold onto things 18–28
    see also decluttering
cobwebs 57
coffee machines 67
coffee tables 245
collectibles 193–4
cooking utensils 101
cosmetics 84, 98–9, 133, 159–60
cots 243
crockery 101–3, 167, 232
cutlery 101, 167, 232

deadline-setting 35–6
decluttering 7–11
   and grief 28–9
   knowing where to start 7, 46, 79
   motivations for 28, 36, 38, 90, 222
   positive change of 121
   setting a date for 221
   shared responsibility of 10–11
   and the *Sort Your Life Out* process
      15–41, 43–73, 75–117, 119–211, 213–32
   and staying organised 215, 221–3
   and support organisations 251–2
   see also letting go
decorating 151–2
descaling 62, 63, 67
designated places, for every item 128–9
digital detoxes 202
dishwashers 65, 167
displaying items 24, 114, 131, 148, 193–5, 207
divorce 39, 115
donation 21, 82–3, 99, 104, 110, 222–3, 250–1
drawer organisers 148, 172
drawers 238–9
   bedroom 136–48
   kids' 173
   kitchen 168, 172–4
   stair 245
duvet sets 187–9
DVDs 106, 107, 195

electronic devices 106, 108
emotional attachments 18, 22–4, 38, 85, 113–15, 201, 206–8, 220
Ex Test, The 115

fabric stashes 25
feature walls 241
filing systems 198–201
fireplaces 242
floors, cleaning 59, 60, 70
folding
   aprons 182–3
   clothing 136–47, 153–5
   duvet sets 187–9
   fitted bed sheets 190–1
   tea towels 179–81
   towels 161–5
food banks 104

food items 103–4, 175–9, 216
freezers 65, 167, 176
fridges 65, 167, 176
furniture
   bedroom 131
   flexible 246–7
   with hidden storage 245–6
   living room 68, 193
   oversized 247, 249
   upcycling 237–41

gadgets 21
garages 204–6
gift experiences 217
glassware 101, 172, 232
greeting cards 208
grid systems 111–12
grief 21, 28–9, 252
grout 62

habits, ditching old 216
hand-me-downs 156
handbags 148
handles, disinfection 58
hanging systems 171, 243
headboards 243
hoarding disorders 31, 252
hoodies 138
house clearances 28–9
house plants 71

in-trays 200
indecision 19, 24–5
ironing boards 185

jeans, folding 140–1

kids 38, 99, 109–10, 194–7
kitchen appliances 52, 66–7, 100, 175
kitchens
   cleaning 65–7
   sorting 100–3
   systemising 166–83
   upcycling 239, 243
   work triangle 166
knitwear 134, 138

labelling 51, 129, 206
   clothing 149
   food 176

paperwork 198
toys 197
laundry 156, 186
lazy Susans 173–4
letting go 28–9, 34, 38, 40, 53
    easing yourself into 83–4
    following up on decisions 92
    power of 15, 31
    and sentimental items 22, 85, 109, 113–14
light fittings 57
light switches 58
limescale removal 62, 63, 67
living rooms 68, 106–8, 192–6
lofts 204–6
log burners 71

make-up stains 61
mattresses 61, 187
maybe piles 89
MDF, moisture-resistant/green 244
medicines 161
memory boxes 24, 201, 208, 220
memory quilts 207
mental health 20, 251–2
microwaves 66
mirrors 59, 63, 240
mobile phones/chargers 108
money issues 16, 18, 21
motivation 28, 36, 38, 90, 222

notice boards 178, 197

offices, home 111–13, 197–203, 248
ovens 66
overwhelm 18, 21, 38, 83, 85, 196

painting 238–9
pans 171
pants 142–3
paperwork 111–13, 198–203, 222, 232
pegboard organisers 199
photographs 114–15, 193–4, 206
picture hanging 194
polishing 68
purpose 48, 50–3

quilts, memory 207

radiators 58

recycling 50, 82–3, 96, 107–8, 110–13, 250–1
relationships, impact of clutter on 15, 16, 31
renting 25, 217
repairing 96
repurposing 96, 101, 103, 207, 237, 243, 248–9
room dividers 193
rooms
    functionality 124–7
    layout 127
    room at a time approach 51–2
    Sorting by 94–113
    Systemising by 131–206
    zoning 124–5, 150–2, 167, 192–3, 195
    see also specific rooms

scanners 203
sealants 62
selling stuff 21, 25, 82–3, 92, 222, 250
sentimental items 18, 22–4, 38, 85, 113–15, 201, 206–8, 220
shelves, floating 148, 193
shoes 50, 94–6, 148, 245
shopping
    bargain hunting 216–17
    bulk buying 184
    compulsive 21
    decision chart for 218
    duplicates/multiples 99
    impulse buying 216–17
    one-in, one-out policy 219
    overbuying 10, 21, 99, 175
    rules for 215, 216–19
showers 62
shredders 112, 113
shutters 57–8
sinks 63, 66
socks 146–7
sofas 68, 71
Sort 43, 75–117
    by category 45–7, 49–52, 80–1
    checklist 116
    comparing and discarding 87
    following up your decisions 92
    room by room to 94–113
    and sentimental items 113–15
    and storage space 86–91
    and The Ex Test 115

Sort Your Life Out process 13–41
    golden rules 33–41
    Sort 43, 75–117
    Staying Organised 213–33
    Strip 43–73
    Systemise 43, 119–211
space
    assessing your 45, 52–3
    having vision for 35
    marking out 81
spare rooms 204–6
stair drawers 245
Staying Organised 213–33
    cleaning rules 223–32
    decluttering rules 215, 221–3
    shopping rules 215, 216–19
storage 101
    assessing your 34, 86, 94
    bathroom 157–65, 244
    bedroom 94, 132–49, 152–6
    garage 206
    home office 198–203
    innovative ideas 127, 167–8, 235,
      237, 244–9
    interconnected nature 52
    kitchen 166, 167–83
    and labelling 129
    living room 193, 195
    loft 206
    sentimental items 206–8
    toys 152, 196–7
Strip 43–73
    checklist 73
    and cleaning 54–72
    with purpose 50–3
support 10–11, 38–9, 223–6
    lack of 19, 27–8
sweaters 138–9
sweatshirts 138–9
Systemise 43, 119–211
    by room 131–206
    checklist 210
    and functionality 124–7
    and sentimental items 201, 206–8

T-shirts, folding 138–40
tables 246, 248–9
taps 63, 64
tax records 201, 203
tea towels 179–81

therapy 251–2
time issues 18, 19–20
to-do jars 224
toilet bombs 64
toiletries 84, 98–9, 133, 159–60
toilets 63
tongue-and-groove boards 241
tools, renting/borrowing 217
toothbrushes 55, 62–4
towels 96, 104–5, 161–5, 219, 232
toys 49, 109, 152, 196–7, 220
trousers, folding 140–1
tumble dryers 69, 185
TV screens 68

unsubscribing 203
upcycling 24, 151, 207, 235–43
use-by dates 103–4
utility rooms
    cleaning 69–70
    sorting 104–5
    systemising 184–91
    upcycling 239

vacuum-sealed bags 149
vacuuming 59, 70
vinegar 59, 62–3, 65, 67, 69, 71
vinyl, stick-on 239
vision 35

wall stickers, chalkboard 197
wallpaper, self-adhesive 151–2
walls 57, 62, 65, 241
wardrobes 131–49
    capsule 27, 49, 95, 222
    cleaning 54
    floordrobes 149
    going shopping in your 95
    oversized 249
    upcycling 240
    see also clothing
washing machines 69, 185
wealth 31
wedding memorabilia 115
window cleaning 59, 63
wooden furniture 68
workspaces 111–13, 197–203, 248

zoning 124–5, 150–2, 167, 192–3, 195